JUST A BOY FROM LONDON'S EAST END

AUTOBIOGRAPHY

ERIC JAKOB

A FAMILY AND SOCIAL HISTORY

Published in Great Britain 2007 by Eric Jakob
81B, High Street, Ware, Hertfordshire. SG12.9AD.

No part of this publication may be reproduced, stored in a retrieval system, or transmitted, in any form, or by any means, electronic, mechanical, photocopying, recording, or otherwise, without the prior permission of the publisher.

A CIP catalogue record for this book is available from
The British Library.

ISBN 978-0-9555951-0-3.

Every effort has been made to fulfil requirements with regards to reproducing copyright material. The Author and Publisher will be glad to rectify any omission at the earliest opportunity.

(942.1.5.082.92)

Printed in Great Britain by: CALL PRINTERS LIMITED
St Ives, Cambridgeshire. PE27. 3LF.

With Special thanks to my Mother for her unfailing love,

****

To my Dad who knew me,
but unfortunately I do not remember him.

****

To my Grandparents who helped make it all possible for me.

****

And Last, but not Least to my Wife Pearl, for all the Help, Patience, Encouragement, and Support, not only with this Book, but in everything I have achieved, as without her None of which would have been possible.

****

A BOYS LIFE IS HIS HISTORY, FOR WHEN A MAN DIES, A BOOK DIES WITH HIM.

****

No people will look forward to posterity who do not often look backward to their ancestors.

(Edmund Burke)

****

INTRODUCTION

I would like to empathise to any readers of this book, that it is my intention to give a small taste of life for a small boy growing up in London's East End during wartime, and the progression from that time to the 21st Century, which is a completely different world, our education was so different to today, our purpose was firstly survival, which would then show in our achievements, how to fulfil dreams, etc, without any Government Interference, what we got out, is what we put in, and I hope that you will consider the contents of this book in the way I have tried to write it, and excuse any mistakes such as grammar etc, as this is a true account as best as I can remember, and write it.

AUTHORS NOTE:

When Pearl, my wife, persuaded me to write a book, it made me realise just how much I owed to so many people who had helped me through my life and to achieve my ambitions, to review my life brought home to me how lucky I have been, starting in the early part of my life with my mother, who was always by my side, my Grandparents, particularly my Grandad Robinson, who taught me so many things, basic training in business skills, negotiating, buying and selling to make a profit, then came my uncles, and their wives , and of course my own aunts.

No school, college, or university, could possibly give me the real life experience that I had, of course, there were down sides but every down side concentrates the mind to overcome problems and failures, and are the best experience to fulfiling future achievements, I read somewhere once, that the only failure is not to try, and learning by that failure is the best experience for future success, common sense and confidence are at the heart of all business decisions, plus of course good timing.

The wisdom of my Great Grandfather, over 100 years ago, has been passed down to me through the generations, and genes, my thanks go to all my family, with a special thanks to the Headmaster, and teachers of my Secondary Modern School, for the basic education that they provided.

Eric Jakob.

****

THE EAST END OF LONDON

London's East End has always been a place of poverty, and immigration, dating back over many centuries, but with many success stories, and various fortunes having been made by East Enders, and I do not feel that this has ended even in the 21st century.

Three people that I really do admire all started from humble beginnings in London's East End, and went on to make their own fortunes they are ;

        Sir Charles Clore,   (Multi Millionaire)

        Sir Alan Sugar,   (Multi Millionaire)

        Gerald Ronson,   (Multi Millionaire)

I am grateful to Sir Alan Sugar who kindly consented to me mentioning his name in my book, and for his good wishes to the success of the book.

I am also very grateful to Gerald Ronson (Chief Executive of Heron International Group) who wrote to me with further details of his East End connection, his parents were born in London's East End, and his Grandparents were Russian Jewish immigrants.

CONTENTS

1. Early Robinsons 1
2. My Early Life 11
3. Towards the End of the War 29
4. Working with Grandad 37
5. Towards the End of School Day 45
6. Leaving School 51
7. My Mum and Dad 55
8. Jakob Side of the Family 65
9. Meeting Pearl and Marriage 79
10. My Army Day's 89
11. Discovering the Truth 99
12. A Turning Point 107
13. Development Days 113
14. Freemasonry 137
15. Mark (My Nephew) 145
16. Return to School 149
17. Visit to Local School 151
18. Anniversaries 153
19. Acknowledgements 166

EARLY ROBINSONS

To start a story, one should start at the beginning, so where is the beginning of Eric Jakob (with a 'K'), before proceeding with this story, I would firstly like to say at this stage how I consider myself to have been very fortunate and lucky, with perhaps one exception, being without my Dad, which is not an ideal start to any life, however, this was wartime, and although I never remembered my Dad, I have, and still remain very proud of him, and the famous regiment in which he served, which held a gallant stand at the defence of Calais in May 1940, of which was a great assistance in the evacuation of Dunkirk, now all part of history, but I must say that I am particularly proud to have become a member of that regiment.

Now lets go back 3 or 4 generations, not an easy task as will be shown later in the book,

Firstly, on my Mother's side, as this side of the family was the greatest influence on my life, lets start with Great Grandfather, as far as I have been able to find out, my Great Grandfather Alfred, was born in 1851, in Thurfield Hertfordshire, his father was Joseph, a farm labourer, Alfred married Georgina (nee Preston) a servant girl whose father was also a Joseph a Coachman, they married in 1874, in the Congregational Church Thurfield, in Hertfordshire, they had twelve children but not all survived, in fact, 7 died in infancy, with a average life span of 3 years, Georgina died on the 21st January 1897, aged just 42 years old.

My Great Grandfather Alfred, as a young man worked as a driver, horse and cart in those days, transporting whatever was needed in a mainly farming area, it soon became clear to him that he would do better if he worked for himself, so he hired a horse and cart, and began contract haulage work, and apparently made a lot of money, this is probably the first signs of money motivation within the family.

At a later date, the details are sketchy, but we assume he and his wife left the countryside, and made their way to Walthamstow, on the edge of London's East End, this must have been shortly after 1874, as the children were born in Walthamstow from 1875 onwards.

Within a short time, Great Grandfather became involved in house building, and progressed to become one of the areas largest property developers, and over a few years was responsible for large scale developments in Walthamstow, and surrounding areas, being responsible for the building of the landmark lighthouse building in Markhouse Road, he soon became a very wealthy man, and together with a Solicitor, and a Land Agent, they between them formed a local Building Society, to provide funds for the purchaser's of the many properties that they were building, this was at the end of the 19th Century, and the early part of the 20th Century, the building company continued to expand, to the extent of purchasing large forest areas in Canada, they would fell the trees, and ship them back to England, for their own use, any surplus timber would then be sold to timber merchants, and the cleared sites in Canada would then be sold, as cleared sites, at a profit.

My Grandfather, Alfred John, was the second youngest son and was born in Gamuel Road, in 1886, and attended Gamuel Road school, he trained as a carpenter, but because he was quite hard to handle, a tearaway, he would be called today, his

Great Grandad Robinson the founder of our Property Foundations, towards the end of the 1890's.

Grandad Robinson, five from the left in the light coloured suit, taken in July 1909, at Evanston USA, probably on the banks of Lake Michigan.

Grandad Robinson in the middle, just before leaving Canada to come home to England in 1912.

father gave him a ticket to America, (not the best part), and told him he had to work his way home, the ticket was a one way only, it went straight to Panama, where he worked on the construction of the Panama Canal, however, he gradually worked his way north, through America, it took him 12 years.

In about 1906, he became a night club manager in Chicago, at that time, most of the clubs were strongly controlled, I leave it to the reader to understand who was in control, however, it was a very adventurous time for a young man, in a new and expanding Country, and full of opportunity, later on, I have a document signed by Grandad, in 1908 in Buffalo,U.S.A, to become an American Citizen, so that he would be able to work in the dockyards, but, I understand that he would not give up his English Citizenship.

Grandad told me that when he worked on the skyscrapers, he would have to start at the bottom of the ladders in his own time, as he would only be paid from the work place, the climbing the ladders would not be paid for – he eventually travelled to Canada, and then home to England, he used some of the place names in the U.S.A, and Canada in his childrens names, i.e. my mothers name Winnifred, was named after Winnipeg, in Canada, my Uncle Alfred's second name was Evanston, a suburb of Chicago, U.S.A.

When my Grandad returned to England he married my Grandmother Ethel, who had waited for 12 years for his return, they married, and lived, in Walthamstow, where Grandad started to build houses, unfortunately, Grandad was a gambler in his younger days, and this would appear to be why our side of the family remained the poorest, his brothers, George, and Sidney, remained quite wealthy.

My Grandad Robinson taken in Buffalo USA. About 1906.

Great uncle George, was the owner of a large farm on the outskirts of Chelmsford, I remember as a small boy going to his farm, and enjoying the victoria plums from the orchard, Great uncle Sidney, developed vast residential estates in the neighbourhood of Eastern Avenue, Ilford.

Grandad's sister Violet, married very young and had 23 children, but again, not all survived, in her younger days, she and her husband who was an Austrian, together ran the Bell public house in Walthamstow, with a staff of 23, I remember when Grandad and Great Aunt Violet got together, they were very close, and great company always laughter, and great stories mostly funny, and stories about America.

After my Mum was born, and her brothers, my Grandad and the family moved to a Public House in Sandon, Hertfordshire, where Grandma ran the public house, and Grandad had a stall in Royston Market, he employed his nephew Sonny, probably, this was the first in the family of an Uncle and nephew relationship, my Mum, started her schooling in the village school, and had to look after her Brother Alfred, Mum told me that they had great fun and on one occasion, my Uncle Alf was riding a horse, when it galloped off with him holding on for dear life, when the horse stopped suddenly Uncle Alf was thrown over the horses head and landed in the village duck pond, and was covered in green slime, and weed, this was always a laughter point for many many years, eventually, the family moved back to Walthamstow, and over a number of years Grandad had various houses, including a time at Chingford, but it was Walthamstow that became the family home.

My Nana Robinson standing at the rear with members of her own family – probably just before she married.

Nana and Grandad Robinson, my Mum with her doll in front of Grandad, my aunt Joyce next to Mum holding her doll, – aunt Irene, next to aunt Joyce, aunt Irene died in 1941 with Leukaemia, and uncle Alfred far right taken early 1920's.

Grandad Robinson, with his car, and children, my Mum is sitting in the passenger seat.

MY EARLY LIFE

Some of my earliest memories come from when I was very young living with the family, in Grove Road, in those day's families would all live together in one house, with Mother, Grandad, Grandma, Aunts, and some Uncles, as most of the men were away fighting in the war, most of the houses had Air Raid Shelters in the back gardens, these were called Anderson Shelters, and were half buried in the garden, the top half was covered with earth, the shelter inside the house was called a Morrison Shelter, and it had a thick metal top, with a table cloth put on top so it could be used as a table, I also remember my first day at school my Mum took me and I was greeted at the school by my Aunt Rose's younger brother Bill, he was a few years older than me, and he said that he would look after me , this he did very well over those first few years at my first school, bearing in mind this was war time, over the next 60 years or so, when we meet, we still talk about my first days at school, but now he is saying that perhaps it is me that should look after him.

I do remember that there were no lights on in the streets, and we had black out curtain at all the windows, which had to be closed during the hours of darkness, the lamppost, together with any trees were painted with white paint bands. The cars, buses, ambulances, and other vehicles were not able to have any lights on, but they had white paint on the front and rear, the white paint helped to make it safer for the drivers, and of course people walking home in the dark would not walk into lamppost, etc, but of course there were accidents

I think this was my first school photo – I am second row from the front third from the right.

Another school photo – this time I am in the front row, fourth from the right, please note the type and mixture of clothing worn by the children.

Yet another school photo – I am second left, front row, all three school photo's appear to have the same fencing in the background, well, that fence survived the bombing, I can still remember a few of the childrens names, – especially the girls.

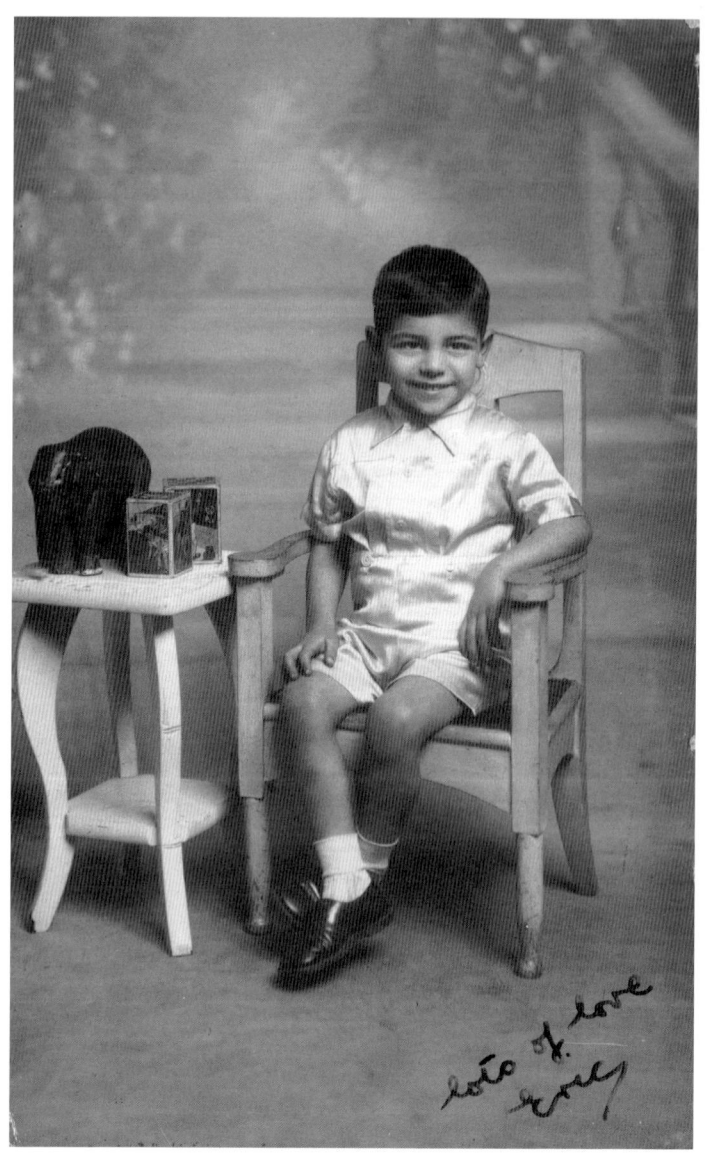

Eric – dressed up as a smart little boy – I wonder where that suit came from ...

As we all lived together in one house, the bedrooms had to be allocated, my bedroom with my mum, was shared with my aunt Joyce, and my cousin Alan, who was younger than me, the bedroom was at the top of the house, a large room with a large dormer window, each side of the dormer window the ceiling sloped, under one side of the ceiling, was my bed, and the other slope was Alan's cot, one day during an air raid, a bomb exploded quite near the house, and part of the ceiling fell in all over my bed, but Alan's side escaped any damage.

When I was home from school, I used to help in the kitchen with my Nan, she would be preparing the dinner for us all, I would cook up all the potato peelings etc in a large pot and cook them on the kitchener (kitchen stove), for the dog, named Peggy, she was a large breed of dog, I do not know what breed she was, but she liked me, probably because I helped to feed her, when we were in the garden I would ride on Peggy's back like a horse, Peggy always growled at Alan, I dont think Peggy liked Alan.

My uncle Cyril (mums youngest brother) who volunteered by signing up for the army under age, when he joined the Berkshire Regiment, he was in the army for about three years, and during that time was transferred to the Seaforth Highland Regiment and spent some time in Northern Ireland after the war, he was discharged, and came home to live with us all, and he worked with his brothers, my other two uncles, I also remember Alan and myself, with uncle Cyril would sit under the table, and attack a tin of condensed milk, Alan and myself would have a small tea spoon, whilst uncle Cyril would have a dessert spoon, but we all enjoyed the milk.

As I was growing up – NOTE MY VERY PRIZED BOOTS.

We did not have any school uniforms, and cloths were made at home with whatever material could be used, shoes had to be taken care of as it was difficult to have them repaired, the boys, I was included, had boots with studs to help them last longer, most of the boy's enjoyed the boots with the studs, as they made quite a lot of noise.

Some time in 1944, my Mum asked me not to play on a small green near our house where we would normally play with some of the other local children, she seemed to have a premonition, I did not know how she knew this at the time, and still do not know, but she said, dont play on that green today, instead, play in the next street, with some other children, for once, I did as I was told, and played in the other street, in the opposite direction from the green, during that afternoon there was a very loud explosion, and plenty of smoke from the direction of the green, my Mum came running out of our house looking for me, but, I was safe, Mum told me after that a Rocket (V.2) had landed on that green, demolishing 2 / 3 houses, and a lot of children had been killed.

Another time, in the late afternoon, I had come home from school, and was talking to some school friends, at the top of the next street close to where I lived, there was a loud explosion and down the bottom of the street, it was covered with smoke, when the smoke started to clear, we could see that there was a great pile of rubble, and 2 / 3 houses had almost disappeared one of the houses is where my friend lived, who we were talking to, he just stood there, a lady who lived quite near, saw him, and picked him up quickly, and took him straight into the doctors house, which was almost opposite where we were standing, he was of course in shock,

Bomb damage in Grove Road, 'Our Road', fortunately, this was at the other end of our Road.

later we found out that his whole family had been killed, that is, his Mother, Brothers, and a Sister, who were all having their tea, he would have been killed with them, if he had not stopped to talk to us, we were told after that the explosion had been another Rocket (V.2).

Some time after, I was standing on the bottom rail of our front gate, with my Cousin Alan, we were watching a doodlebug (V.1) flying bomb, when the engine stopped, we saw it fall, followed by an explosion, this time it was at the top end of the High Street, causing a lot of damage, and many people were killed, I was told many years later that the bodies of some people had to be taken down from the lamppost, or what was left of them.

We would spend most of the nights in the Anderson Shelter, one particular night, Grandad as usual would say that he would stay in his bed, if he was going to die, he would die in bed, but that night, it was heavy bombing, and a bomb exploded nearby, and blew him out of bed, he came running down the garden in a night shirt, and clambered into the shelter, disturbing us all, but it was a funny sight, I can still visualise it, there was an incident, when my Grandma was walking down the stairs and just as she passed the landing window, there was an explosion, and the glass from the window came in and she was badly cut, but in her normal way, she made her way to the kitchen, cleaned up her wounds, and continued as if nothing had happened.

At school, we would start with assembly, this probably helped the teachers in counting the children, to get the correct number that were still attending the school, the Headmaster, with his teachers, would stand on the stage in the assembly hall, where we were all lined up, the Headmaster would start with 'Good Morning Children', and would continue with "unfortunately a few children will not be with us today due to last nights bombing raids", when we got into our own classroom we would look at the empty desk but before prayers, he would ask all the Jewish children to leave the assembly hall and go to their classrooms in an orderly manner, there were never any problems, I dont remember any other faiths at the school, but there may have been, with all the disruptions, of interrupted lessons, some time all night awake in shelters, we still managed to get an education, all without Counselling unlike today, looking back at that period of my life I would not say that we were not affected, we just got on with growing up, we would enjoy our play time in the school play ground, sometimes, if a raid came during school time, we would have to go to the school shelter, but at the end of the day, we would walk home, there were no Mums collecting us in cars in those days, for us children, it was an adventurous time, plenty of bomb sites to play on, windows to break, shrapnel to collect.

All great fun, there were of course, food shortages, in fact everything was in short supply, but most parents knew where to get some extra food, I understand it was called Black Market, "Rations on the top of the counter, Black Market under the counter", I remember some time after the war ended, saying to my Mum "do bananas have pips, as the only bananas I had seen were dummy ones hanging up in the greengrocer's shop, or on the market stalls.

On my birthday, it must have been in 1944, my Mum, got me a three wheel bike, I dont know where she got it from, but I remember riding it round the kitchen, we used to visit my

Results of Rocket (V.2) devastation, this was quite near to us, and it was this type that exploded on the green where I would have been playing.

Top picture shows yet another Rocket (V.2) attack, and the bottom picture shows damage by Bombs.

Results of Bombing in Vernon Road, one can see the belongings of the occupants laid out on the footpath, including treasured bikes, even a child's three wheeled bike, this is the type that I had, and Mum used to ride with me standing on the back.

Two photo's of shelters, top one, the outside Anderson Shelter after a bombing raid, – the bottom photo shows a Morrison Shelter, used inside the property, the occupants were protected when the house was destroyed by a doodlebug (V.1) flying bomb.

Top photo, shows two houses completely destroyed in Greenleaf Road, many years after the war, my Cousin Valerie lived in a house two houses from this picture. The bottom picture, shows Bomb damage in the High Street, where the market was, – and still is ...

Nans who I knew as Nana Jakob, we would go to tea, it was this Nana that introduced me to winkles, shrimps, and salad cream, a liking I have had for the rest of my life, she always buttered (marge of course) the bread before cutting a slice, this was different to my Nan who I lived with, and seemed very strange at the time, I would always enjoy my visits, my Grandad, and Nan would always be pleased to see me, and I could not do anything wrong, I was told much later in my life by my Aunt Connie, who was my Dad's youngest sister, that her Mum and Dad loved me very much, and thought the world of me, perhaps this was because I was the first Grandchild, and that I was very much like my Dad, the son they had lost in the war, there was an occasion, when I went into the chicken run, and try and play with the chickens, this was something my Mum was not very pleased with.

During these visits, I would meet up with my Aunt Florrie, and my Aunt Connie, who were both my Dad's sisters, my Uncle Bill, and Uncle Harry, Dad's brothers, were both away in the Army so I did not see them during the war years, during the early evening, the entertainment was playing dominos, and cards, I remember it was mostly playing crib, when it was time to go home, Mum would ride my three wheeled bike up the middle of the road, with me standing on the back, we had great laughter at this, of course the bike was much to small for Mum.

My aunt Connie (sitting) with my aunt Florie (standing) with two of my Cousins, both of these aunts were my Dad's sisters, this photo was taken after the war.

During my early school days, I was in a Biblical play, I was dressed up complete with headdress etc, I played Judah, who sold his brother Joseph for twenty pieces of silver, the only words I had to say, after stroking my beard (false of course) was "SO BE IT" and my brother was sold, – some people said years later that I had been type cast, – being able to sell my brother without any conscience, I was never in any more plays, and have been told many times, that I still do not have any conscience ...

My aunt Joyce (Alan's Mum) would sometimes look after me whilst my mum was at work, aunt Rose, (uncle Alf's wife) would also look after me, both aunts would clean me up before mum arrived home, but somehow I seemed to get dirty again, just before mum arrived.

After the war about 1948, Mum's house, the one that was completely destroyed in 1940, was rebuilt, but Mum had to start repaying the mortgage all over again, right from the start, also the general rates on the property, (today, the general rates are called Council Tax), but there were no concessions for war widows in those days, Mum had to pay the full amount, and it was about this time that I started to understand mortgages, – mortgage payments, etc, Mum had a struggle with all the payments, but none were ever missed,
Mum received 2/6d (37.5 pence today) per week for me and this was paid by the Regiment, no allowances from any Government Source's in those days, and the 2/6d stopped on the day I started work, my 15th birthday.

TOWARDS THE END OF THE WAR

Towards the end of the war, I had three Uncles working on bomb damage building work, we all lived together, and at the end of the day, they would come home have a cup of tea, before taking the truck back to the yard, they had converted an old motor car into a truck by cutting off the back part of the car, and building a truck on the rear part, before taking the truck back to the yard, they would say do you want to come for a ride, as a small boy this was not to be missed, my Cousin Alan, would also want to come, this was O.K. except when it was raining, Alan of course being younger than me would sit inside the cab, I would have to sit on the open back of the truck, but who cared, once the truck was put away, we would all walk home, and have our tea.

Uncle Lewis told me that when Grandad was working on bomb damage work, he would use an up stairs front room which was usually the largest room in the house as a workshop, where he would have his bench etc, one day, the foreman said to uncle Lewis, your father seems to be a bit slow, uncle Lewis said back to the foreman, "go and tell dad", the foreman went inside the house, and up the stairs to where grandad was working, uncle Lewis of course stayed outside the house, he heard the foreman talking to grandad, the talking got louder, and louder, then came the sound of footsteps very quickly running down the stairs, the foreman came running out of the house first, with grandad chasing him with a saw in his hand, uncle Lewis could not stop laughing, – he would never had approached grandad in that way, although, uncle Lewis would be very hard to handle he would normally hit first, and then calm down, but this was the type of environment that I was being brought up in, stand up for your self especially if you feel that you are right.

Another occasion, with uncle Lewis, was, that he would go to the timber yard at lunch times to collect timber and materials, he was very well known to the manager of the yard, one particular day, he arrived as normal, but the manager was not available, so he was seen by a new member of the staff, uncle Lewis asked for his order, and was told to wait, with this uncle Lewis just hit the man, one blow, and knocked him out perhaps it was the way he had been spoken to, - uncle Lewis told me later that he never again waited for materials, and he had an apology from the yard manager.

Probably, you had to be like that in those days.

At the end of the war, I went to the usual street parties, but what I do remember was that the men were gradually coming home from the war, I suppose that this was the first time I realised that my Dad, would not be coming home, my school friends Dad's had returned, my Uncles had returned, I remember my Uncle Fred, Alan's dad, coming home, he had been in the navy on the Russian Convoys, I only remember seeing him once during the war, it was quite funny, he came home, knocked at the front door, Grandad answered it with a greeting of "hello Fred when are you going back", it was not until 1946, that my other uncle Fred came home from Burma, – he was a "Chindit", *(the Legendary Special Forces Unit)* and had a very bad time in the war, this was the first time I had seen him, he brought me home a Burma hat, the type the Australians wear, with one side turned up, for some reason I took to him, and he took to me, he told me later, that he never knew my Dad, but had left a lot of friends back in Burma,

Me standing on top of the Anderson Shelter, with uncle Alf's and aunt Rose's dog, just after the end of the war.

Top photo, uncle Fred, and aunt Myrtle's wedding, I am the page boy, Alan by my side, with our Grandad looking over us. – Bottom photo, me in my page boy suit eyeing up the bridesmaid.

who like my Dad, would not be coming home, who also had small children like me, perhaps, he was thinking of them when he saw me, he was quite tall, and he used to get on his knees and taught me how to fight, he probably taught me some of the things he learnt in the army, I was never bullied at school, perhaps because of what he taught me. After a while, this uncle Fred married my aunt Myrtle, one of mum's sisters, and we all lived together in the same house, Uncle Fred, and Aunt Myrtle had one room on the first floor.

I particularly remember this wedding, the wedding breakfast was prepared by my Mum, and my Aunts, as it was still very difficult as food was still in short supply, and food rationing was still in force, but a good spread was made, I remember all the food was taken to the hall on a barrow boy's open barrow, and we all pushed it through the streets to the hall, laughing all the way, I was a page boy at that wedding, all done up in a page boy's suit, with a bridesmaid on my arm.

After a while things started to get back to normal, so I was told, it was all very new to me, no more sleeping in the air raid shelters, watching for doodlebugs etc, and the bomb sites gradually disappearing, I remember Alan and myself, used to play on a bomb site that used to be a school building, the main walls were still standing, but the roof, first floor, and ground floor had completely gone, all of these were in the basement area many feet below which was all burnt pieces of timber, and rubble, with most of the timber sticking out and pointing upwards, – someone before us had climbed up the building and tied a large thick rope to a remaining beam at the top of the building, this in turn was left hanging down for all to play on, I, Alan, and many other children would swing on this rope across the open basement area, what great fun we all had, we did not appreciate the danger if we had fell off the rope, I shudder to think about how dangerous that all was. Alan and me would go to the local swimming baths at Leyton, (now a large Tesco supermarket), I was quite a good swimmer, I dont remember how, or when, I learnt to swim, - however, Alan at that time could not swim, - I would be in the water at the deep end as this was the end where the diving boards were, Alan would climb the ladder to the top diving board and then just jump off into the water, as near to me as possible, I would then pull him to the side and this would be repeated many times, we enjoyed this as great fun, I just think what great confidence Alan as a small child who could not swim had in his Cousin, – but thats how we grew up, we all relied on each other.

My Grandad, would take Alan and me to the local pictures to see the eight cartoons, during the filming, Grandad would fall asleep, Alan and myself would move away, then when the films ended, Grandad would wake up in a start, he would shout out "where am I", we would kill ourselves laughing, but the next time he took us he would sit in the middle of us and hold our hands, so that we could not move away from him, Alan and me still remember some of the cartoons from those days, we speak about them all these years later and still laugh, to particular ones that always come to mind, are 'Mustard makes the meal' and we have come to borrow a few nick nacks,' there would be the normal Tom and Gerry, and of course Laurel and Hardy, we laughed at them then, and Alans Grandchildren are still laughing at Laurel and Hardy, as did Alan's Son before them, Grandad also would take us to the local Pie and Eel Shop, at Bakers Arms, or in the High Street, (Manzies Shop) the one in the High Street, is one of the remaining eel shops still going all these years later, Alan did not like eel's but instead would have pie and mash with liquor, I loved eels from that time, and still enjoy stewed eels to this day, talking of eels, I remember my Mum, taking Alan and myself to Manzies eel shop, we were all enjoying eating, when Mum suddenly said that she had broken her tooth, Alan and me could not stop laughing, to us young boys it seemed so funny, but not for Mum.

Other things that comes to mind whilst writing this book, is that our food was stored in a food safe, this was normally a fairly large wooden framed box, with a hinged door, covered with perforated zinc on the sides to allow air to pass through, also in the food cupboard, was a cold shelf, which consisted of a concrete shelf covered with ceramic wall tiles, no deep freeze or fridge in those days, the bath was a long and narrow type and was galvanised and when not in use in front of the fire, was hung on a hook in the back yard, the hot water had to be heated on the kitchener (kitchen stove), after the war had ended, my aunt Joyce and uncle Fred (Alans Mum and Dad), moved into a new prefab, this was a prefabricated single storey building made in sections in a factory and then assembled on site,these were produced at the end of the war to help with the housing problems, it was estimated to last for about 10-15 years, but I understand that some prefabs are still occupied after nearly 60 years, it was quite an experience, with its own front and back gardens, the kitchen was fully fitted and contained a built in fridge, they were the first in the family to have a fridge.

My uncle Alf, as I recall, was the first in the family to have a television, it was a 9 inch 'Bush', with a large magnifying glass over the screen, so different from today's flat screened televisions.

A new Cousin 'Christine' being held by my Mum, – with Alan, and myself looking on.

My Nana and Grandad Jakob, this is mostly how I remember them.

WORKING WITH GRANDAD

When I was between 9 and 10 years old my Grandad took me under his wing and then started a long and hard training period, of which I did not realise at the time would be be grooming for the rest of my life, Grandad would start his teaching in his own way, he was very Victorian, and would not suffer fools gladly, he would tell you once and expect you to grasp it straight away, I got on very well with Grandad, maybe because I did not have my own Dad, who knows, but I shall aways be very grateful to him.

When Grandad purchased houses, they all required refurbishment, and it was me that usually was the first in, start clearing, one of the first jobs, was to clear out the coal cellars, I had to collect any coal that had been left, then sift the coal dust, ready to make into coal blocks, next saw up any old timber and then chop into fire wood, after the house had been cleared, one of my jobs was to make a mixture of Creosote, and Spirit of Salts, and then treat all the timber areas against woodworm, particularly under the staircase, and floorboards.

On some occasions, I had to go to the local builders merchants and hire a builders barrow, for 1 shilling per day, (5p) the wheels were almost as big as me, this was for collection of sand, cement etc, and clearing any rubbish.

At one particular house Grandad was selling, there was a damp patch under the front window, that afternoon, a purchaser was due to view the house, Grandad, and I went to a local furniture dealer who he knew, and purchased a large dresser, with strict instructions that it had to be delivered within the next hour, Grandad paid £2.10s, for the dresser, the purchaser viewed the house and confirmed the sale, when he asked about the dresser, Grandad said he would leave the dresser in the house for £5.00, the dresser was sold there and then, a good profit.

Another occasion, I remember, Grandad bought a house and took me there to clear it, he just gave me the key, I thought it was still occupied, as there were still the plates, cups etc on the table, and the house was full of furniture, and personal effects, I thought that at any moment the owner would come in the door, I was later told that the owner had died, and Grandad had bought the house as it stood.

It was not long before I was joined by my Cousin Alan, 3 years younger than me, we both enjoyed working together, Grandad would say to us both, "do you want 3d or 6d per hour, we would look at each other, and then say 6d please Grandad, he would reply by saying have 3d per hour for being greedy, next day, same question, 3d or 6d per hour, we again would look at each other, bearing in mind the previous day, and not wanting to appear greedy, we would say 3d please Grandad, he would look at us and say have 3d per hour for not speaking up for yourselves, we could not win, other times, Alan and myself would have a laughing spell, Grandad would say I dont pay you to laugh, we could not stop, so we said we would continue to laugh, and not get paid, A BIG MISTAKE, we worked for nothing that day.

I remember mixing concrete, by hand, (no mixers then) Grandad would knock the stones of the gravel which had rolled to the sides with his walking stick, and say dont waste the gravel, this used to annoy me, also when I had to pull all the tacks or nails out of floor boards, I would clear one board at a time, up one board, down the next so that there were not any missed, Grandad would come into the room, and say you have missed these boards, I would reply, that I have not yet reached that board.

I did not realise at the time, but this was all hard training, Grandad was teaching me, he once showed me a plan of a house, and said what is wrong with the plan, I studied the plan, and said I could not find anything wrong, he quickly said "no airbricks in the bedrooms", I was only 12 years old but never forgot the lesson, (to day airbricks are not fitted in bedrooms, but this was before central heating).

ADVICE FROM GRANDAD, he once said to me, "Do not ask me for any money, as I will not give you any", but I will teach you how to get it", another lesson not to be forgotten,

Each week I had to fill in a time sheet, Grandad knew exactly how many hours I had worked, when I asked him why I have to fill in a time sheet, he just said, I know how many hours, but do you know, a lesson for the future.

Later on, Grandad started taking me to property auctions, a very interesting place for a young boy, I was told to sit, watch, listen, and learn, and do not interrupt whilst the bidding was going on, I did sit, watch, listen, and learn, a lesson that proved its self over and over again in later years.

Auctions were the place to be, I remember years later, when Grandad wanted me to take him to an Auction somewhere in the country, unfortunately, for some reason I could not make it, about three weeks after, I spoke to my Grandad, and asked if he went to the auction, and did he buy a property that he was interested in, he said, that he bought the property, and also some other properties that formed almost the whole street, he also said that he had since sold them again in another auction room, this was called "turning the contract", another lesson learnt.

Another business that Grandad was engaged in was that he would buy houses that were occupied, he would pay the occupant a sum of money, and they could stay in the house until they died, after that the house was sold by Grandad, today many Insurance Companies, and Mortgage Lender's now carry out this type of business, Grandad would tell me how it all worked, and this was probably the first time that I understood the word, Equity, the value on the balance sheet.

Perhaps in some way, when I look back now, I say to myself was this the time that I started to realise what Grandad was doing for me, for example, checking house plans, – filling in time sheets, – learning how to make money, – going to auctions, – etc, – etc.

I am now convinced that this was all beginning to fall into place, for a future, of which at that time, I was unaware of.

Me and my Mum, ... What else is there to say ...

My Nana Robinson towards the end of the war, which shows the strain of providing and running a family home during the war years, – Note the carpenters stool she is sitting on.

Nana and Grandad Robinson, towards the end of the 1940's.

A treasured photo of my Grandad taken in the 1950's.

TOWARDS THE END OF SCHOOLDAYS

When I was about 12 to 13 years old, and not working for my Grandad, my Uncle Harry, my Dads brother, used to pick me up in his tipper lorry, and he taught me to drive his lorry across the gravel pits, this was my first time at driving, about the same time, in the evenings and after school I used to work on the local Fairground with two of my friends, my job was to strap the girls into the dive bomber, if they screamed whilst on the ride, the operator would stop the ride, and I would then join the girl, or girls, and somehow the screaming would stop, my friend Bob, would work on the dodgem-cars, and Jimmy who was only 15 years old would work in the boxing booth taking on all comers from the crowd, they could earn £3.00, if they lasted 3 rounds, not many lasted 2 rounds, but they thought that they would last as Jimmy was only 15, and not very big, but they were wrong, Jimmy later went on to own his own night club in London, Bob and myself with Jimmy used to belong to the local boxing club as most boys did in those days, but more often Bob and myself played snooker mostly for a penny a point, we made quite a lot of money, in fact we soon learnt how to Hustle, after a good night at the snooker club, we would get the bus and go home ready for school the next day.

Our school was a Secondary Modern with fantastic teachers, some of the teachers would finish their training at our school before going on to teach in reform schools, they thought that the training they had at our school was some of the best they had, our Headmaster, was superb, and always put his boys first, he used to say that his boys would never stave, how right he was, but he did have two rubber stamps in his office, for when we were ready to leave school, we would be called to his office, where he would stamp our foreheads with either Failure, or Car Dealer, depending on how well we had done with our school work, my stamping was car dealer, perhaps a good sign for the future..

There was no bullying at our school, if two boys were seen as starting bullying, they were quickly taken to the gym, put on boxing gloves, then into the ring, after a good bashing, they would be the best of friends, perhaps, this should be encouraged today.

Our maths lessons were very good, the teacher would be writing on the blackboard with his chalk, – suddenly, he would turn to the class, he would point to one of the children and ask very quickly 3 x 7's, quickly came back 21 Sir, the teacher would turn and continue writing on the blackboard, suddenly he would again turn to the class, 16 x 3's, just as quick would come back 48 Sir, back to the blackboard he went, until a wrong answer was given, then as quick as a flash - first the chalk, followed by the blackboard rubber, straight at the child who got the wrong answer, – where did these teachers learn to be such good shots, but the children were just as quick, ducking out of the way – Was this intended to teach us how to duck and dive?

Our Headmaster would always praise his boys, for their achievements in boxing, swimming, etc, we did have all England schoolboy boxing, and swimming champions from our school.

I took a great interest in Maths, and used to go for extra teaching at my Maths teachers house some evenings, numbers have always interested me, together with history.

On one occasion, Bob and myself, decided miss the afternoon at school, and go to the local cinema which was at the bottom of the road to our school, we sat down, and the film started, it was not long before the film was stopped, with this happening, Bob and myself went quickly into the toilets, and then the lights came on, we heard our Headmaster on the stage, his school was quite empty, and of course he knew where his pupils were, so he had all the boys, and some girls, leave the cinema and he marched them all back to the school, we came out of the toilets, and enjoyed the film.

These were good times, good school, and good mates, my Grandad used to call my mates dustbin boys, a name that stuck for many years.

I do remember one evening, at a local dance hall some trouble started not unusual, this time the police were called, we left the club, and walked about 100 yards away, with this a boy from our school and the club, ran passed us and disappeared under a road bridge, straight after him came a policeman, and a black maria, (police van), they could not find him, I said to the policeman, "the long arm of the law, and a weakling gets away", he was not amused, he grabbed me, and Bob, put us into the police van, we then spent the next 3 hours in a police cell, then released, and by this time we had to walk home.

Some evenings, we would go and sit in the local highway cafe, with other older boys, there was always an attraction of cars, mostly Ford V.8's, 22 & 32, Buicks, Studibakers, etc, all black with white wall tyres, except the Ford Pilot's they were always Green, I am sure that many deals went on in that cafe, and lots of problems, between the various groups, I was again very lucky, never any problems, I had a older boy named Charlie, from Bethnal Green, I was told after that he was the brother of the Infamous Twins, he took a shine to me, and looked after me, this was especially helpful to me where the snooker payments were involved, I never had any problems in collecting, there were times when we visited South of the River, (Thames), but only by invitation, as this was know as crossing the border from the East End, and then we would only go in groups of at least 3 - 4 strong, in those days, Docklands, was still the docks, and with its scrap yards, and scrap yard dogs, all so different from today's up market Docklands.

Around this time, there was trouble between two rival gangs, a leader of one of the gangs had returned home, when he had a visit by two members of another gang, they knocked at his front door, and when he answered it the two pushed there way in, and chased him up the hall way and started to beat him, he put up his hands to protect his face, as he did so, his hand was severed at the wrist with one blow of a short sword, he was eventually taken to the local hospital but had lost his hand completely, no one of course knew who had done it, but there was no more trouble between the gangs. This was all about 1954, and all part of growing up it was at this particular time of my life that it would have been so easy to become involved in crime, and this may have been a road that I may have taken, after all, some of my mates at that time became involved with criminal gangs, but fortunately, I didn't, my Grandad, and both my uncles Alfred, and Lewis, were there to provide an alternative, after, I believe my mum had spoken to them.

Between the ages of about 13 years up to 15 years, was a very good time of my life, I had many girlfriends, in fact, three particular different girls, on different days of course, a girl would come home with me from school, and light the fire in the dining room, you may draw your own conclusions, but the fire had to be lit, and burning well before my Mum came home from work, and fire lighting was part of my job, this was possibly the first of my delegation skill..

When I was 15 years old I had which I thought a steady girl friend, her father took a liking to me, and would run me home in the evenings on the back of his motor cycle, on one occasion, I was on a bus going to see this girl it was a Sunday afternoon, on the same bus was my friend Bob, he was going to the snooker hall, and said would I join him, as it was still quite early I said yes, so I stayed on the bus, and played snooker for the afternoon, and we did quite well for money, it was now early evening, when I arrived at my girlfriends house, I was quite pleased, but when she opened her front door, she said where have you been, I said playing snooker, and we now had some extra money to go out to the pictures or whatever, she promptly told me to continue playing snooker and not to see her again, I do believe this was the first and only time I had been dumped.

Taken with uncle Cyril and aunt Doris, & maybe a girlfriend.

Mum, Grandad, and another girlfriend.

LEAVING SCHOOL

I left school at 14 years old, this was because leaving school for me, was at Easter, which was at the beginning of April and the school closed for the Easter holiday and would not reopen until after my 15th birthday, so, when I left, I was only 14 years old..

I did however get a job on a building site before actually leaving school, I was asked if I could start work on the Monday, but I said I could not as it was only the 12th April, and I would not be 15 until the Wednesday, I started work on the Wednesday, my birthday, but by the Friday, I had, had three different jobs, so I did my first deal on the Friday, by selling back my insurance stamps, as I had three for the one week, and only one was required to be put on my insurance stamp card, my Mum was very upset, as to the start of my working life, however, I did settle down in my third job.

After a while I went to work on another building site, this one was building an extension to a Convent, which was also part of a Girls School, my job was as a tea boy, one of my duties was to buy the tea, sugar, cakes, rolls, filings, etc, and to generally look after the workmen on site, I soon saw the potential of this job, I would select a grocers shop, bakers, and a butchers, in those days mostly independently run, it was not long before deals were being made, for example 15 rolls for the price of 10, cakes etc on the same basis, bearing in mind this was repeated business every day for the shop keepers, ham, cheese, meat, etc, all the same, good profits were to be made, and on top of that I was getting paid as a tea boy, the Nuns quickly for some reason took a liking to me,

Mum and Me taken on a seaside pier.

they would provide dinners for the workmen, I, as part of my job was to take the numbers required, collect the dinner money for the Nuns, and for this I was provided with a dinner without any cost, and as a bonus there were the school girls, who I got very friendly with, perhaps another story.

When I was 17 years old, I passed my driving test first time, this was because I had the driving experience from both my uncles, mostly my uncle Alfred, and my uncle Harry in those early days driving his lorry over the sand pits, I bought an American Ford Mercury Estate car, a large 9 seater, from a car dealer in Bow, uncle Alfred came with me, on the way home the car broke down, the driver of the car following me started very noisily to shout and sound his motor horn, he did not realise that my uncle Alf was directly behind him, uncle Alf got out of his car, walked up to the side of this noisy person and quickly sorted him out, suddenly, and very quickly the noisy person pulled out and sped up the road, probably he thought for the best, with the help of uncle Alf, we soon got the car going again and sorted out the problem, another occasion with this car is when I took a girlfriend out one evening, and we went off road, (not many four wheel drives then) however, the car got firmly stuck in the mud, so we had no alternative but to leave the car, the next day when I went to work I asked the groundworkers on the site, if they would come that way home and pull me out with their lorry, you can imagine the embarrassment to the remarks of the men when they saw where the car had got stuck, but it did not take long for them to get the car free, in those days, there would be about 10/12, ground workers to each lorry.

At about that time I was stopped for speeding, and of course off to the local Magistrates Court, the chap in front of me was also before the Magistrate for speeding, the Magistrate asked him if he had anything to say about why he was speeding, the chap replied that if he was late for work, he would lose half an hour off his pay, the Magistrate replied well you have just lost £2.00, next, it was then my turn in the Court, same question from the Magistrate, but my reply was, I do not have any thing to say, with this the Magistrate said, " £2.00 for you as well".

Another treasured photo of my Mum and Grandad, the two people in who really influenced my life.

MY MUM AND DAD

I cannot proceed much further with this story without the mention of my Mother, who was a very exceptional and courageous Lady, she was born in the early part of 1916, in Walthamstow, she was the first of seven children, life for her was very hard from the start, she had constant moves in the early part of her life, Walthamstow, to Sandon, in Hertfordshire, then back to Chingford, and back to Walthamstow, her up bringing was very strict, and as she was the eldest in the family, it was expected and did in fact consist of helping to bring up her brothers and sisters, together with constant helping of her mother, she told me that in her teenage years it was very difficult to go out and enjoy herself as teenagers do today, she had to wait for her father to go out first, and then slip out herself.

She had to work for her father, in her spare time, (if she had any) but she made the time her job was letter writing etc, it was on one of these occasions, in posting letters that she met my father, a love that lasted for the rest of her life, my Mother and Father married in 1936, she was only 20 years of age, this was now the happiest time of her life, their first home was a flat in Walthamstow, eventually after nearly three years of hard work, Mum and Dad bought a new house, and then I was born, it appeared that Mums life was now complete and happy, with a new house, and her own family, unfortunately this was just pre-war, and in May 1940, my father was killed in action, Mums life was shattered, and in addition to that in October 1940, the house was bombed by a direct hit, and completely destroyed, with the loss of every thing, including many wedding presents some not even opened, my Mum and

My Dad taken about 1932.

myself were at my Grandparents home, where we remained for the rest of the war.

When my Mum met my Dad, there were three boys who used to sit on the kerb, and wolf whistle her as she went by, all three boys died the first one died when the Submarine 'Thetis" sank in Liverpool Bay in June 1939, the Thetis was one of the greatest tragedies in the submarine service, my Dad was next to die in Calais in 1940, and the third boy, died on H M S Hood in 1941.

The last time mum saw my dad was on the 10th May 1940, this was of course the last time he saw me, apparently I walked towards him taking some of my first steps, - I often think about children who's fathers never saw them, or even knew that their wives were pregnant what a terrible loss that must be for the children that did survive not knowing that their fathers did not even know that they were on the way.

Mum never got over losing my father, but Mum being what she was, and a small boy to bring up, faced the future with her strong and determined attitude, she was determined to be both Mother and Father to me, providing most important love, and as time went on we became even more close, she was always there for support, as I gradually got older, and the war continued, I started at a infants school, and mum went to work, in a local factory, where she would do piece work in order to try and earn extra money, as in those days money was in very short supply, there were occasions when Mum at the end of a week would take the bus to work, for part of the journey, and then get off the bus and walk the rest of the way as she did not have enough money for the whole fare, but she never gave up.

My Mum and Dad, when they were both young and courting.

My Dad

My Dad just before World War 2.

My Mum and Dad's Wedding.

The three of us in happy days for Mum and Dad - with me in the middle – But War was just around the corner ...

Me on my Dad's knee, the last time Dad was home – before leaving for France, – Note the Anderson Shelter in the background.

On one occasion, I remember, I came home from school on the Friday, and said to mum, that we were going to learn long division starting on the next Monday, Mum sat down over that weekend and taught me how to do long division, by the time Monday came, I knew how to do long division, my teacher was very impressed, but I said that it was all down to Mum, this was the type of lady she was, even in those day's nothing was to much trouble for her, of course over that particular weekend she would have had so much to do, after working all week, but she made the time for me, as usual.

THE JAKOB SIDE OF THE FAMILY

My Great Grandfather was Ludwig Jakob, who was a external decorator in Germany, his job was the decorative plasterwork on the external walls of buildings, he left Germany in 1886, with his Wife Marie, and lived in London's East End near the Collins Music Hall, my Grandfather Charles Ludwig went to the nearby schools, and later on would swim at the Roman Road Swimming baths, and obtained many swimming certificates, my Greatmother Marie died in the German Hospital in 1901 she was aged only 43 years of age, during the first World War Great Grandad was interned and spent the remainder of the war in an internment camp, this was because of his German name, it was during this time that he change his name to Palmer, so after the First World War had ended, and he was released, he was known in the family as Grandad Palmer, this was all long before I was born.

Grandfather Charlie who for some unknown reason did not change his name, he was in his younger days a blacksmith, but later on he became a bouncer at the local public houses, today, he would be known as a doorman, although not a very tall man, he was extremely strong and very well set, on one occasion, and after some trouble, it took six men to hold him down, however, I understand he was very good at his job, and was always in great demand for his services.

Grandad's first wife died in 1911, leaving Grandad with a small 7 year old son, soon after, my Grandad met my Nan at a fairground, Nan, who was only 20 years old when she married in 1912, had been working in service, she was, as I understand a very rebellious type of person, when she was

My Great Grandad Jakob who changed his name to Palmer during his period of internment during the First World War, – he is seen here with his second wife.

My Great Grandma Jakob, Grandad's mother, she is the one standing.

My Grandad Jakob, an early photograph.

working, one of her jobs was to clean a large front room carpet in those day's before vacuum cleaners, it was cleaned by beating, and brushing, the lady of the house said to my Nan there are sardines in the cupboard, for your lunch, with this my Nan replied "I shall need more substantial food than sardines if you expect me to work as hard as this" I also understand that she walked out of that job shortly after.

When I was about 15 years old, I began to ask questions about my roots on my fathers side of the family, but this always seemed to be hushed up, it took me almost 50 years to find out where my Jakob roots had come from, so working hard, before such things as the Internet, many visits to London Archives etc, a break through came in 2002, I managed to get hold of the 1901 Censors my Great Grandad, Great Grandmother were clearly shown but disappointingly, showed that they were born in Germany, (no help) – but my Grandad had entered the name of the place he was born, – a breakthrough at last, the place was Metz, Germany, another problem, Metz today is part of France, so I managed to get the help of a local language school teacher who was most helpful, in fact she said she would enjoy helping as she considered this to be a project for her, she translated a letter that I had composed into French, and I sent my letter off to the Metz Archives, – I was delighted to receive not only a response, but a copy of my Grandad's Birth Certificate which showed his fathers and mothers places of birth in Germany, from this I was able to obtain a Marriage Certificate, and further information including the villages that both families had come from, further correspondence was made with the local Burgermeister of the village, a very helpful person, who very lucky for me spoke and wrote very good English.

My Nana Jakob, just before she married in 1912.

My Grandad Jakob when he was about 16-18 years old, note the style of dress, complete with cane and gloves.

Grandad Jakob at about the time of his marriage to my Nan.

After a time I set off in 2004, Pearl by my side as usual to visit Germany, and to fulfil a lifetime's ambition, to find, and walk, in the same places as my Ancestors, – we drove down to Dover, crossed the channel into Calais, with a visit to the Calais war cemetery, although my father does not have a known grave, we always visit and pay our respects to the chaps of the Regiment that are known to be laid to rest in the cemetery.

We travelled through France and then into Germany, a strange feeling crossing the border, is it part of one's Gene's I ask?

Our first stop was Saarbrucken, quite a nice hotel, we settled in and then went for a walk, and visited a local Pub, inside the pub, on the walls were many prints showing the old parts of the town, and the surrounding area's of many years ago, I was of course very interested and this must have shown to the Inn Keeper, and some of his customers, again, I was lucky, the Inn Keeper spoke English, and was over the moon when I said that my family had come from the area, and that I was tracing my roots, in fact long conversations were being had by all, with the Inn Keeper translating to his customers, we all had a good evening.

Next day we made our way to Kirkell, the village that my Great Grandfather lived, all now newly rebuilt after three wars, 1870/71, 1914/1918, and of course 1939/1945, we found a hotel, where no one spoke English, but fortunately a local baker was in the hotel at the time who spoke English, so we made our requirements known, and no problems, the Housekeeper was a very nice and traditional German House keeper, who did her very best to try and understand us, Pearl had already prepared her notes in German from a German dictionary, she would write in German what she wanted and show the writing pad to the house keeper who then understood, Pearl is very good at this and all went very well, I was extremely happy with the hotel it was really traditional German, with its furniture and decorations etc, and for some reason I felt at home.

Next day, we went to the Burgermeisters office that I had been in correspondence with, what a charming person, he really put himself out to be as helpful as possible, we went to the local Archives, and found copies of Birth Certificates, Marriage Certificates etc of the Jakob family dating back to 1776.

I could not believe that I was now in possession of all this information, something that had not been known to any members of the family for almost 100 years.

The Burgermeister, arranged, and presented to me copies of all the documents, a problem was that of course they were all in 'Old German', and all showed at the time to be in the Kingdon of Bavaria, now Southern Germany, this was all before the unification of 1871, he also presented to Pearl some village gifts.

The next day we walked around the village, speaking as best we could to the villager's I was quite surprised how many people spoke English, or tried very hard to do so, we had the normal cream cakes and tea, and enjoyed the company of the people, who were very interested to learn that my family had originated from this particular village, at last we visited the oldest ``part of the village, which included an old castle, I thought this must be the place to walk where my ancestors would have walked all those years ago.

I must say that, the Saarland, is a most beautiful part of Germany, with its pretty houses, and scenery etc, the whole place is kept very clean and tidy, Pearl did comment to me why did your ancestors leave such a beautiful place for the East End of London towards the end of the 19th Century? of course I have no idea how to answer that, maybe another story.

When we arrived back in England, I contacted the German Embassy in London, who put me in touch with a German translator, who was able to translate my documents from 'Old German' into English, these documents are now a very treasured part of my belongings, and I feel that I have achieved another one of my ambitions

I would like to say at this point that after trawling through the various documents, I found that Great Grandad's second wife came from Edmonton, – My Grandad, (both of these were Jakob's), first wife also came from Edmonton, this was in the early 1900's, many years, and two generations later Pearl, my wife, also came from Edmonton, – just coincidence, – who knows.

The Jakob Coat Of Arms

And Its History

Coats of Arms were developed in the Middle Ages as a means of identifying warriors in battle and tournaments. The present function of the Coat of Arms (although still one of identity) serves more to preserve the traditions that arose from its earlier use.

Heraldic artists of old developed their own unique language to describe an individual Coat of Arms. The Coat of Arms illustrated herein was drawn by an heraldic artist from information recorded in ancient heraldic archives. Our research indicates that there are often times a number of different Coats of Arms recorded for a specific surname. When possible we select and translate the Coat of Arms most representative of your surname or its variant for illustration.

THE JAKOB COAT OF ARMS HEREBY ILLUSTRATED IS OFFICIALLY DOCUMENTED IN RIETSTAP ARMORIAL GENERAL. THE ORIGINAL DESCRIPTION OF THE ARMS (SHIELD) IS AS FOLLOWS:

"D'AZUR A DEUX SOCS DE CHARRUE ACCOSTES ET ADOSSES D'ARG., EN PALS, LES POINTES EN BAS."

WHEN TRANSLATED THE BLAZON ALSO DESCRIBES THE ORIGINAL COLORS OF THE JAKOB ARMS AS:

"BLUE; TWO SILVER PLOW BLADES PLACED SIDE–BY–SIDE AND BACK TO BACK WITH THE POINTS TO BASE."

ABOVE THE SHIELD AND HELMET IS THE CREST WHICH IS DESCRIBED AS:

"THE PLOW BLADES WITH THE POINTS TO TOP."

THE JAKOB COAT OF ARMS.

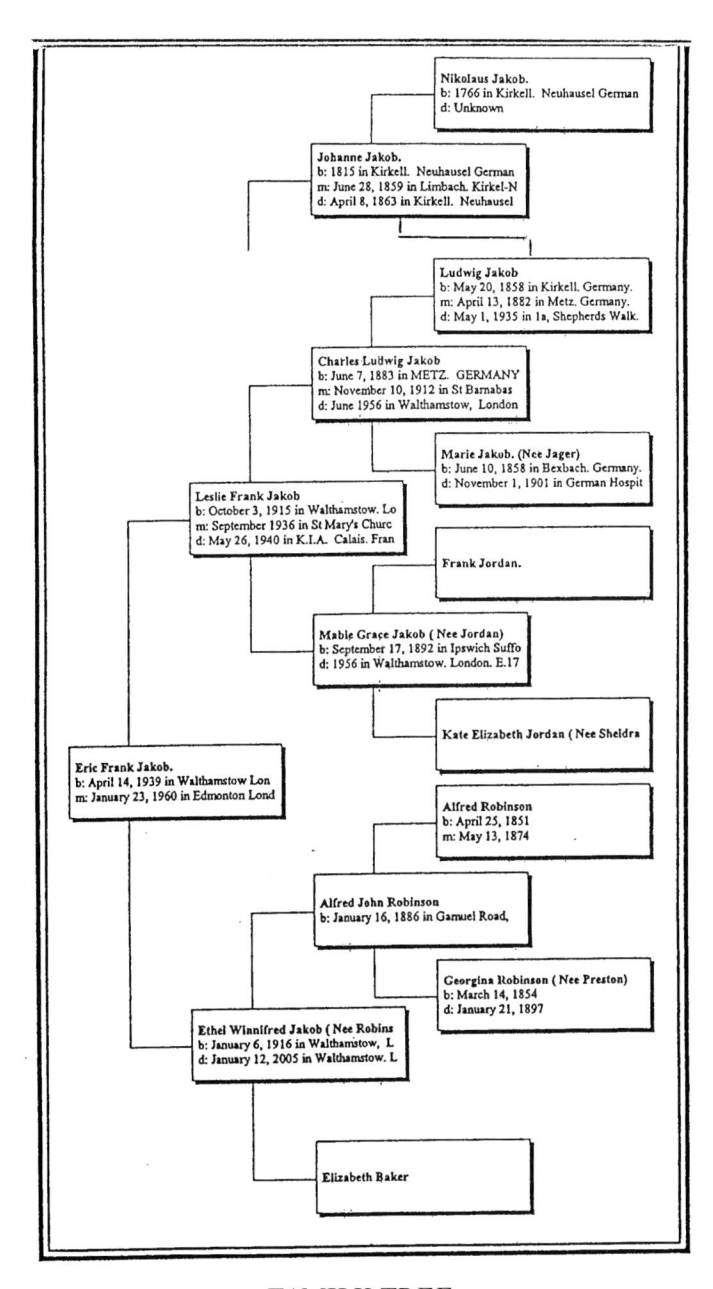

Nikolaus Jakob.
b: 1766 in Kirkell. Neuhausel German
d: Unknown

Johanne Jakob.
b: 1815 in Kirkell. Neuhausel German
m: June 28, 1859 in Limbach. Kirkel-N
d: April 8, 1863 in Kirkell. Neuhausel

Ludwig Jakob
b: May 20, 1858 in Kirkell. Germany.
m: April 13, 1882 in Metz. Germany.
d: May 1, 1935 in 1a, Shepherds Walk.

Charles Ludwig Jakob
b: June 7, 1883 in METZ. GERMANY
m: November 10, 1912 in St Barnabas
d: June 1956 in Walthamstow, London

Marie Jakob. (Nee Jager)
b: June 10, 1858 in Bexbach. Germany.
d: November 1, 1901 in German Hospit

Leslie Frank Jakob
b: October 3, 1915 in Walthamstow. Lo
m: September 1936 in St Mary's Churc
d: May 26, 1940 in K.I.A. Calais. Fran

Frank Jordan.

Mable Grace Jakob (Nee Jordan)
b: September 17, 1892 in Ipswich Suffo
d: 1956 in Walthamstow. London. E.17

Kate Elizabeth Jordan (Nee Sheldra

Eric Frank Jakob.
b: April 14, 1939 in Walthamstow Lon
m: January 23, 1960 in Edmonton Lond

Alfred Robinson
b: April 25, 1851
m: May 13, 1874

Alfred John Robinson
b: January 16, 1886 in Gamuel Road,

Georgina Robinson (Nee Preston)
b: March 14, 1854
d: January 21, 1897

Ethel Winnifred Jakob (Nee Robins
b: January 6, 1916 in Walthamstow, L
d: January 12, 2005 in Walthamstow. L

Elizabeth Baker

FAMILY TREE.

My Mum taken in 1976.

MEETING PEARL AND MARRIAGE

In October 1957, I met Pearl who was to become my wife we got engaged in 1958, after I had asked her dad for his permission to marry his daughter, this was the custom in those days, he asked the usual questions, "would I be able to keep his daughter, and where were we going to live, what are my future prospects" I had great difficulty in answering, as, at that time, the future was not all set out in front of me, but he understood, and agreed to the engagement, and we married in Edmonton in January 1960.

My uncle Alfred, who was always very close to me, he was like a brother, and he gave me the usual Fathers talk, before getting married whilst walking round the block with me, which did help at the time, he was also my best man, and he got on so well with Pearl.

I considered that I had chosen very wisely, I am not sure what Pearl thought at the time ... or since ..., However, my choice has been proved right many many times since we married, I reflect what a great investment I had made since 1960, there have been many up's and down's, especially in the early years, when we had little money, but as my headmaster had said all those years ago, we did not starve.

Pearl was able to manage on the small money that I gave her, she would go down to the local High Street, and buy a small joint of meat which would last mostly for the week, on Sunday, we would have roast, Monday, cold meat, Tuesday, mince meat, Wednesday, meat pie, all from the same joint Thursday, sausages, and egg and chips on Friday. Pearl was a

Pearl when I first met her 1957.

Pearl when I first met her 1957.

My early bricklaying day's taken on top of a building showing a typical bricklaying gang of 6 and 3.

Me at about 18 years old when I was leaving Pearl's house.

Pearl and My Wedding Day, 1960.

Cake cutting at our Wedding.

very good manager, she had been taught well, coming from a large family on a small income, but we managed, things were hard for us at that time.

When we were first married, I would be working as a bricklayer, if it rained, there would not be any work, and therefore, no money, I would give Pearl the house keeping money as best as I was able, but when there was work, good money could be made, she paid the rent, as we were renting two rooms in Stamford Hill at the time, the two rooms were at the top of a large house, which was owned by a Jewish family, very nice people, but the mother would catch me on my way in, and keep me talking for which to Pearl seemed to be for ever, we eventually moved from there, and went to live with Pearl's mum and dad for a while, after that we lived with my mum for a while, and then through Pearl's Aunt we were able to get a rented two bedroom flat, and we settled down for a few years.

About this time I was working for a Irish sub-contract bricklayer, who had his office in the corner of the bar in a public house at the back of Camden Town, at the end of the week he would sit at a small round table in a corner and pay out his men, most of whom would then spend their money at the bar, but I didn't, we all worked on what was called the lump in those days, earn your money, and move on, – I remember working on Finchley bus garage for another brickwork sub-contractor, I recall that I laid 2,500 bricks in a day, that ment lifting two and half cubic yards of cement mortar on my trowel, without even laying a brick, my fingers had to be taped up with insulating tape each day to prevent the skin from wearing away, but good money was had, again, make your money, and move on, this was the way of the lump.

The middle 1960's, these were very hard times I had a major financial disaster, I was still very young, and quite inexperienced, but managed to overcome the problems firstly, by not walking away from them, definitely not my style, – I put my head down, and worked my way out, I do admit now that I did sail a bit close to the wind on many occasions, but that was all part of my up bringing, and training, although not apparent at the time, but it paid off.

Many years later I was told by my cousin Brian, uncle Lewis's second son, that his father would come home and say "I dont know how my nephew Eric sleeps at night with some of the stokes he pulls" and this coming from uncle Lewis, – thats rich ... How did he sleep?

Money was in very short supply, Pearl was marvellous, always there for support, and encouragement, but on one occasion, Pearl stood bail for me, I dont remember why I was on bail, or perhaps I dont want to remember, many years later Pearl told me that she was in two minds at the time whether to pay the bail or not, mainly to teach me a lesson, but who knows, fortunately, it was never required.

Pearl and me unfortunately did not have any children, but perhaps this was for the best, I must say that I have been rewarded by marrying into a large family with many caring nephews, and loving nieces, and now with the increased number of great nephews, nieces, and great great nephews, and nieces.

Our Wedding day, unfortunately the weather was unkind and it rained all day.

MY ARMY DAYS

In 1960, I had just got married, when I had to go and commence National Service, but again I appeared to have struck lucky, firstly, I was sent to Aldershot, and carried out my basic training, then, after a few weeks, I was transferred to Yeovil, in Somerset, on a motor base, with a vehicle park containing over 4,000 vehicles, as I was quite a good driver, I was excused many of the daily driving duties, I would have to line up the vehicles in the parking area, which allowed me to take a vehicle out of the camp, drive around the countryside, and then return to the park and leave the vehicle in the correct position, – then the next vehicle, and so on, so that by the end of the day the vehicles were all neatly lined up.

After a short time at the camp, I asked the C.O. if I could bring my own 12 seater van to the camp, I explained that it would be useful to transport the chaps to and from the local dances etc, held in the adjoining villages, and of course, allow me to take the van fully loaded to London at weekends, which of course was to my advantage.

The C.O. agreed, he thought it would be a good for morale, and that his boys would get back to camp in good condition, as he agreed, and I was on my way out of his office, he said to me "do you come from the East End of London", I said yes Sir, he then insisted that I do not park my vehicle any where near his petrol pumps, - what was he implying -.

Pearl has often said, "what did you get your national service medal for", I always answer, for ensuring that morale was kept high at the camp.

HILL 60.
YPRES 1915-17.
SOMME 1916-18.
ARRAS.
SCARPE 1917.
CAMBRAI 1917.

VILLERS-
BRETONNEUX.
AMIENS.
HINDENBURG LINE.
FRANCE & FLANDERS
1914-1918.

Q.V.R. GAZETTE

THE JOURNAL OF
QUEEN VICTORIA'S RIFLES
The King's Royal Rifle Corps.

HEADQUARTERS:
1st Bn., 56 DAVIES STREET, W.1.
Mayfair 1875.

B. Coy., 27 LYMINGTON ROAD, HAMPSTEAD, N.W.6.
Hampstead 4841.

2nd Bn., 39 GROSVENOR SQUARE, W.1.
Grosvenor 3565.

Published by kind permission of Colonel H. V. Combe, D.S.O., M.C., T.D.

No. 3   JULY 1939
Price 6d.

Front page of Q.V.R. Regimental Journal 1939.

Marriages

Sgt. E. Groves to Ruby Edith Cordle, 27/5/39.
Bugr. S Stace, to Gladys Campbell, 20/8/38.
Rfn. L. Le Grys, to Mary Leach, 12/6/39.
Rfn E. Nance, to Nina Lilian Maud White, 29/4/39.
Sgt. H. T. Baldock to Eileen Ida Grace Ball, 16/7/38.
Rfn. E. White, to Stella Violet Harrison, 27/2/39.

Births

L/Cpl. C. Golding, a son, Michael Liddiard, 29/10/38.
Sgt. A. West, a son, Stephen Arthur William, 1/4/39.
Rfn. L. Jakob, a son, Eric Frank, 14/4/39.
L/Sgt. E. Woolley, a son, Robert, 7/10/38.
Rfn. T. Kirkup, a daughter, Margaret Crowe Davidson, 9/1/39.

Death

We regret to record the death on the 24th April, 1939, of Rfn. F. A. Burt.

OFFICERS' MESS

The outstanding feature of the Officers' Mess has been the pleasant duty of welcoming new officers. To those who remember past difficulties this has provided a most remarkable contrast to the state of affairs not so very long ago.

Many of the new officers are of course being posted to the 2nd Battalion and a special, though unofficial, welcome to Lieut-Col. H. M. Butler, M.V.O., M.C., its new Commanding Officer, was arranged by Col. Combe. Lieut-Col. Butler, who himself served in the 60th, will have the help of some officers of that regiment, than which nothing could be more suitable. He will also have Major Dickins and six other officers transferred from the 1st Battalion and two old Q.V.R. Officers of whom Major Farrer will be second-in-command. There will also be three officers who have served with us as Riflemen (who are most welcome), whilst the others include representatives of such diverse units as the Scottish Horse and the Royal Navy. The latter is presumably an insurance against further unexpected conversions. But from wherever they have come, we are glad to see them all.

Arrangements are being gradually made for the formation of a 2nd Battalion Officers' Mess. Indeed it is already in existence, and the relationship which it is hoped will always animate the two units was expressed by a resolution carried gladly by a combined meeting of both Messes "that as a permanent measure, all Officers shall always be members of the Mess of the other battalion."

My first mention in a Regimental Journal placed by My Dad in 1939.

Front page of the Queens Regimental Journal 1967.

D Company, 5 QUEENS

First notes from the new D Coy. will naturally be tinged with nostalgia for the "Old Regiment," so you must excuse us if we cry "DieHard" occasionally

However, with the New Year, comes the new Regiment and a great challenge for us all. The main issue will, of course, be recruiting, which must be tackled with full enthusiasm. The first weekend's training under the newly-organised battalion takes place shortly when other companies of A.V.R. III do battle with ourselves for supremacy in the skills of fieldcraft, weapon training, etc. Our honour is at stake.

Crying "Die-Hard" once, we must report that in the recent escape and evasion "Fly by Night" exercise, run by the 1st Bn. The Bedfordshire and Hertfordshire Regiment (T.A.) three teams from D Coy. swept the board, and out of about 100 teams, won the first unit prize, beating the S.A.S. into second place. The three teams were led by Cpl. Roger Davis, who has now suddenly become 2/Lt. R. Davis, having recently passed his "board"—congratulations. Other members of the victorious teams were Cpl. Jakob, L/Cpl. Edwards, Ptes. Ockwell, Dodd, Bickerstaff, Wallace, Fox and Symonds.

Another addition to the chiefs has come in the form of 2/Lt. R. Crosher from the Queen's Own Royal West Kent Regiment. Mr. Crosher has taken over No. 1 Platoon from Lt. M. Muirhead, who has gained membership of that exclusive band of robbers called Support Platoon.

We are looking forward to next week's training (!) which will be in the form of a period of drill, followed by a period of T.A. bounty payment, followed by a look at, and a talk on, the Victoria Cross recently acquired by the Middlesex Regiment. The medal was won by our late member, Pte. Edwards. This will be followed by a farewell presentation to Capt. Don Jones and a long period of beer drinking.

If we recover from this strenuous activity we will be having our annual dinner and dance the week after.

More news after the Alka-Seltzer.

N.B. Since going to press we are happy to report that we won the Battalion training trophy.

Another mention in a Regimental Journal 1967, winning the escape and evasion exercise, beating the S.A.S. into second place.

My army day's at the end of a long day's climb.

and at last we reached the top.

Army day's, Getting ready to set off on patrol.

Please do not get the impression that my army training was just driving, and lining up vehicles in the parking area, I was very fortunate to be trained in unarmed combat of which I took a great interest in, and became good at, we were all instructed that we must never use what we had been taught, in civilian life, as this would be seen as a criminal act, but I do remember being taught that the knee joint only bends one way, ... "Think about it" ...

On one occasion, Herby, my brother-in-law, who had recently finished his National Service, were sparring together in a friendly way, when I hit him with a fairly light blow – he stopped sparring straight away, and said "where did that come from" – I apologised, – unfortunately, Herby had difficulty in moving his neck for about three days, we often laughed about that for many years after, and he said that he would not report me ...

Herby, worked for me for a number of years, and we became very close, after all he was my brother-in-law, one day I asked him to throw me a wrench, and as I went to catch it I somehow missed and it hit me on the face just below my eye, my face was badly cut, so I had to go to the local hospital, Herby drove, and when we arrived at the hospital, the Doctor said "how did this happen", Herby said "I threw a wrench at him", the Doctor was quite surprised to learn that Herby was my brother-in-law, but he understood that it was not meant to be on purpose, ... Herby said after ...

"All square now after the sparring incident" we both laughed.

First leave home in 1960.

DISCOVERING THE TRUTH

For almost 40 years after the battle in Calais in 1940, where my Dad was reported missing, and presumed dead, he does not have a marked grave, I could not accept that a person could just disappear, but, of course, we all know in wartime this is only too possible, however, with the regiments help at their London H.Q, they 'discovered' some documents which had been sent from a P.O.W camp in 1941, from a soldier who was with my dad and was with him when he was killed, with this information, I made contact with him, and arranged to meet him, Pearl and myself, made our way down to Eastleigh in Hampshire, we were welcomed by the old soldier who was in a wheelchair, he and his wife made us very welcome, he said that he was really pleased to meet me, he told me about the battle and of the day that my dad was killed (26th May 1940) he knew that my dad had a small baby boy, and now after all those years he had met with me and gave me the exact details of my dads death, he said to me, and this was confirmed by his wife, that he had carried this memory in his mind for all those years, within a short time after our meeting, I found out that he had died, but, from the time of our meeting, and learning the facts of how my dad had died, cleared another part of my strong feeling to discover the truth.

What I learnt on the day of my meeting at Eastleigh, also gave me a much more understanding of the battle, and its importance to the survival of England at that time, much has been written about Dunkirk, and the evacuation of the British Expeditionary Force's, but, Calais, does not appear to have had the attention which it deserves, perhaps, because it was a much smaller part of the main battle at the time.

I would, and feel most privileged, to quote from a paragraph written in the book –

"Brief History of The Kings Royal Rifle Corps – the 60th Rifles" with the kind permission of the Royal Green Jackets Museum Trust

THE DEFENCE OF CALAIS IN CONTEXT

The Defence of Calais was, by any standards, heroic against a backdrop of chaos, confusion and uncertainty, outnumbered, outgunned, and with their backs to the sea, the British, with three Green Jacket Battalions at their centre, plus 800 valiant Frenchmen, held a German panzer division at bay for the best part of three days. Hurriedly despatched, lacking all arms support and without hope of evacuation, officers and soldiers alike fought with a tenacity, courage and gallantry, which, ever since, have provided an example to others. That it was possible, is a reflection upon the high morale and determination of individuals not to fail their comrades or their Regiment.

The strategic importance of the Defence of Calais has often been argued. Churchill was in no doubt that it contributed to buying vital additional time for the subsequent successful evacuation of 360,000 Allied troops from Dunkirk. Sir Anthony Eden, Secretary of State of War, and a former 60th officer, also identified its significance when he signalled to Brigadier Nicholson on 25th May "Defence of Calais to utmost is of vital importance to our Country and BEF and as showing our continued cooperation with France. The eyes of the whole Empire are upon the defence of Calais and we are confident you and your gallant regiments will perform an exploit worthy of any in the annals of British history".

The human cost, borne by so few for the benefit of so many, was high, 300 British troops were killed and 700 wounded. 130 members of the Regiment's two battalions died, including 11 officers. Only a handful escaped. The majority faced five years in prisoner of war camps, which included Brigadier Nicholson, who did not survive, Furthermore, the British had lost the manpower and expertise of two motor battalions. Calais, though. will always be remembered as one of the finest hours in Regimental and Green Jacket history.

****

The Regiments have amassed a staggering 913 Battle Honours, with an even more staggering 59 Victoria Crosses.

I have enclosed on the next two pages copy letters my Mum received, one from Buckingham Palace, signed by H.M. King George, and the second sent by the Regiment.

****

In 2005, Pearl and myself, attended the 250th anniversary of the Regiment at Winchester, a really beautiful day – I again had the opportunity of chatting to a few of the remaining soldiers from the Calais battle, now well into late 80's, but still very proud men, what a privilege for me to be in such company, the event was very well attended, and the icing on the cake was by the attendance of the Queen, as Colonel-in-Chief of the Regiment, taking the salute, my Dad would have been so proud, as I was on that day.

BUCKINGHAM PALACE

    The Queen and I offer you our heartfelt sympathy in your great sorrow.

    We pray that your country's gratitude for a life so nobly given in its service may bring you some measure of consolation.

George R.I.

Copy letter sent to my Mum from Buckingham Palace.

WHERE IS MY DADDY?

TOYS bring new joys—but these little girls are still asking, "Where's daddy?" They are the children of men of the Queen Victoria Rifles who took part in the defence of Calais and are now prisoners of war. South African Voluntary Services sent them toys, and Mrs. Waterson, wife of the High Commissioner, distributed them at a party at St. George's Institute in London.

As far as I am aware, this appeared in a National Press News Paper, Headed "WHERE IS MY DADDY" some time after the battle at Calais, of course, I am not one of the girls, – but one of the boys

The following letter was received by MAJOR - GENERAL SIR JOHN DAVIDSON, K.C.M.G., C.B., D.S.O., Colonel Commandant 2nd Battalion, The King's Royal Rifle Corps, from the Private Secretary to H.M. The King :—

BUCKINGHAM PALACE.

5th June, 1940.

My dear General,

The King, as Colonel-in-Chief of The King's Royal Rifle Corps, has learned with pride of the heroic action of the 2nd Battalion and The Queen Victoria's Rifles at Calais, which assisted so materially in the successful evacuation of the British Expeditionary Force. Such self-sacrifice and gallantry are in keeping with the highest traditions of his Majesty's Regiment and mark a glorious page in its history.

I am desired to assure you of the heartfelt sympathy of the Colonel-in- Chief with the relatives of all ranks of these two Battalions in the great anxiety through which they are passing.

Yours very sincerely,
(Signed) Alexander Hardinge

Copy letter sent to my Mum from the Regiment.

The Rededication of the Calais 1940 War Memorial which took place on the 20th May 1998, after standing on the dock side for over 40 years, the service was conducted by an ex- RGJ, assisted by a Chaplain who was with the 1st Bn R.B. in May 1940.

Me laying a wreath in the Calais War Cemetery.

Me and my Mum on a visit to Calais, which of course included the War Cemetery.

A TURNING POINT

Towards the end of the 1960's, I worked for a development Company as a Site Agent, on one occasion there was an argument between a bricklayer, and a groundworker, both of these men were large built Irishmen, Pearl's dad who was working with me on this site came into the site office and told me what was happening, apparently the bricklayer was about to start laying bricks, when he noticed that the concrete foundation was not level, and he would have to cut each brick of the first course, the argument continued to get very nasty, with both men in the trench, the bricklayer with his back against the side of the trench, and the groundworker standing over him with a shovel at his throat, threatening to slice his head off, I jumped into the trench and parted the two of them, I said, "if any slicing of heads on my site, I would be the one to do it" all so different from today, both men calmed down, and I told them both to leave the site straight away, Pearl's dad could not believe that I had jumped into the trench and parted these two large Irishmen with me not being that big, but I did have the respect of all the workers on the site, and of course, I had to control the site in the best way that I knew.

Within a short period, I worked my way up to a Contract Manager, eventually, I was to be trained for a Directorship of the Company, I spent time in the various departments, i.e. Sales, Marketing, Architect's, and most important Finance, during this time, I was sent to a Merchant Bank in the City for a 6 weeks training course, each morning, we would meet in the entrance lobby with the Chairman, who would greet us with Clapping his hands, – taking a big sniff in the air, saying "Today I smell Money, so lets go and get it". I could not have wished for better training, and the people that were training me, were the same type as myself, we thought, and acted in the same way, what luck to be trained by such people –.

After a while, things were becoming more stable, and in 1969, we moved out of London, and bought a new house in Buntingford, Hertfordshire, we were there for 9 years, and were quite happy, there was one problem, that I was working in London each day, and Pearl was left on her own, and she did not drive, which made it quite a lonely place for her.

In the very early part of the 1970's, I was loaned by the Company that I was working for, to assist as a Contract Manager to a Jewish Property Developer, he was a self made millionaire, and on one occasion I was very privileged to meet with Sir Charles Clore, a multi millionaire, who was also brought up in the East End of London, he may not have been university-educated, in fact he was educated in London's East End, however, he quickly grasped any opportunities that came along, he was the son of a Russian Jew who fled Latvia because of anti-Semitism, and made a living from the textile trade, and small property deals, I was told that Sir Charles was involved in the building of the famous Pan-Am building in New York, and when he could not find a hotel to buy in London, he built one instead, the Park Lane Hilton, – what a man, – a few months before his death, which I learnt later, he was still doing deals, in fact one of the largest land deals at the time, during my meeting with him, he said to me "never lose your East London accent, and remember, be proud of your roots".

In 1973, I purchased a site in Essex, with the full knowledge and approval of the Directors of the Company that I was working for, in fact I purchased the site from them, which was financed by the Merchant Bank that had previously trained me, so I left the Company and set up my own development Company and commenced with the building of 14 houses, the development went very well, and I had sold 13 of the 14 houses, before the market started to collapse due to the world oil problems, however, the Bank agreed to a 4 month extension on the loan, I managed to sell the last house within 3 months, and we were all delighted, my credit rating had now taken off.

I would like to mention that at this time, Pearl cleaned all the houses when they were finished, this was called a builders clean, and with the money that she made by cleaning, of which she worked very hard, and her cleaning was first class, she saved and later purchased stock so she could have her own home sales parties, any further money that she made, she would not spend, she saved it and eventually opened her own shop, (one which she rented from me) in 1980, Mark our nephew helped in the decorations of the shop including putting up the shelving etc

Just before Christmas 1980, Pearl opened her shop, with all the stock fully paid for, and with her own determination, and hard work, she made a great success of her own business.

Before the end of the 1970's, I was contracting, by building blocks of flats, for two of the Directors of the development Company that I had previously worked for, we had kept in close contact, this was of course quite helpful to my cash flow, during this time, I was also engaged in the removal of Squatters from properties, we would be paid £100.00 per house, to clear it, and because of its success it soon attracted the notice of developers, and estate agents, and became quite profitable at that time, I also became involved in contract work with another developer, mostly conversion work, who offered to me a building plot in Southgate North London, in fact, there were two plots, I did a deal with them, that I would have one plot for myself, and build them a house on the other plot on a contract basis, this was agreed, so I was able to build a 3 bedroom detached house for myself, at the same time as building the other house, all went very well, and both houses were completed, I then sold my house at Buntingford, and we moved into our new house in 1979, Pearl was so delighted, she was now back in London, near her Mum & Dad.

Our newly built House in Southgate North London

When I was building my house in Southgate, one of my carpenters who just happen to be Irish by the name of Jack asked me for the door furniture as he was about to hang the front door, I gave him the hinges, and locks, he asked for the letter box, I said to him that I was not having a letter box, (in fact the letter box was to be incorporated in the front gates at the end of the drive), but Jack did not know this, he asked why I was not having a letter box, I told him that if you do not have a letter box you would not get any bills, he was greatly impressed, and said that he would take his letter box off when he went home that evening.

The next day, towards the evening, I returned to the site, and asked Jack if anybody had been during the day, Jack said yes, a smartly dressed man with a suit and tie, and he said to Jack, he had come about Paddy O'Doors, Jack said the man looked like a Tax Inspector, and promptly told him there's no one by the name of Paddy O'Doors on this site, in fact, the man had come to measure for the patio doors, he came back a few days later and we all, including Jack had a good laugh, thats Irish humour, but true.

I would point out that in my days on site, and my own developments most of the labour on building sites was Irish, they were very good and hard workers, and the tradesmen were well trained in their various jobs, i.e. bricklayers, carpenters, plasterers etc, and of course groundworkers, today quite different, most of the Irish labour now work in Ireland, and in many cases English workers now work for the Irish in Ireland, when I speak to developers now as I do on occasions, they tell me that a lot of tradesmen are now Polish, – not much has changed, – only the nationality.

Two of the houses that I purchased and converted into flats.

DEVELOPMENT DAYS

1980–1982, I was currently engaged in a programme of purchasing unmortgageable houses, and converting them into flats and maisonettes, particularly suitable for first-time buyers – both young couples and single people. Flats and masionettes came into their own and were providing as good an investment for the purchaser as buying a house. When I purchased a property, it was completely gutted out and completely remodelled, resulting in a pleasant, comfortable basic home which was of good mortgageable standard, acceptable by Building Societies, and Banks, damp-proofing and timber preservation in old houses is of the utmost importance, and I employed a specialist company to deal with that aspect of the conversion.

I considered that it was right in preserving the friendly terraces of houses that still had many years of life. A typical conversion would have the benefit of central heating, fitted carpets, and would have been completely rewired to provide ample number of power points, kitchens were well equipped with built in ovens, hobs, stainless steel sink, and wall tiling, I also installed coloured bathroom suites, then the entire property was completely redecorated internally and externally.

The converted flats were several thousand pounds cheaper than unmodernised houses at the lower end of the scale, this became quite a sucessfull business, and after a while I managed to secure the attention of a Merchant Bank.

I decided in the first part of the 1980's to expand the business, and formed a small group of companies, the development

Properties being purchased before conversion or refurbishment.

A house refurbishment project, during work being carried out and the finished building.

company was going from strength to strength, I was now developing new build blocks of flats, as well as the conversion of properties, which now included old factories, and a church into flats, which included one of the first churches to be converted into flats, 1983, saw the opening of the first Estate Agency to meet the growing need within the group for its own residential property outlet.

This was after nearly two years of careful planning, the first office was built from scratch and running within eight weeks.

Expert staff were drafted in and their aim was to provide the most comprehensive and professional service offered in Estate Agency, not only selling property, but providing mortgage instructions, via the Building Society links, arranging deposit loans, and liaising with Solicitors, and Surveyors. The Halifax Building Society, the world's No 1 Building Society at the time, were very keen to establish early and secure links with the Agency.

Other branches were quickly established , and as with the first, each one had been chosen not only for its sales potential, but also a great deal of consideration had been taken into account for the comfort and ease of parking for its clients.

The company soon saw the need for a Commercial Department, and soon after, established a department within one of the offices, with a growing register of shops, offices, and warehouse space available. Along with the Halifax other Building Societies were keen to set up links with the Agency, the Woolwich, and Walthamstow soon became established within the branches, and the Agency Company saw further expansion in North and East London, with one office opening in Hertfordshire, the Agency company grew to 10 offices by the end of the 1980's.

Due to the high success of the Estate Agencies, a Financial Service Company was set up to handle the expanding mortgage business, which included house deposit loans, Commercial loans, and Investments, also to identify and secure loans for other Developers.

With all this activity I decided to form my own Finance Company which would specialise in secured loans for Mortgage top up, Second Mortgages, Home Deposit loans, and Property Finance up to 100% for land, and construction cost with participation, to include a package deal, which incorporated a feasibility study, valuation, cash flow, and final marketing.

About 1984, I named one of my blocks of flats "Alfred Place", after my Grandad, and with the use of the newly formed finance company deposit loans / top up loans, I could provide a scheme for first time buyers to move in straight away for only £99 deposit, which was in its self very successful, I did not realise at that time, that I had done practically the same as my great grandfather almost 100 years before, was this purely in my gene structure? ...

During the middle to end of the 1980's the group employed about 25 specialist staff who were active in Property Development, Property Investment, Estate Agency, Mortgage, and Property Finance, the Group's annual turnover was in excess of £5 million, with a portfolio of investment properties growing at a planned expansion rate.

It was at this time, in 1984, that I purchased my Rolls Royce car, I took Pearl and Pearl's dad with me to collect the car, Pearls dad was so proud to be the first to ride in my new car, unfortunately Pearl's mum had just passed away in March, and I did not collect my car until April, Pearl's mum of course would also have been so proud to ride in a Rolls Royce.

It was also about this time that I was in negotiations with the local council at Highcliffe in Dorset, to purchase Highcliffe Castle and refurbish the main structure of the building, and convert into luxury apartments with new build apartments within the grounds overlooking the sea, negotiations went fairly well, and we were about to finalise the deal, when the council decided to withdraw at a very late stage, perhaps, a change of council control, I was never really given a full explanation.

I have since that time made a few visits to Highcliffe Castle to find that the council did in fact retain the building, they hold exhibitions in part of the building, and have tea rooms in the grounds, it would appear that they have carried out some refurbishment works, but up to 2006, the works have still not been completed.

Low-cost one and two bedroom Flats.

A front page of one of my many brochures showing development.

Launching of a Show Flat in October 1980 by the Mayor and Mayoress with Property Developer Eric Jakob.

The first phase of this development consist of 23 units refurbished from the original structure of the old building, and was completed by the end of the year, the second phase which was started in the new year included a further 10 units, with planning permission to build a further 35 units on land at the rear of the property.

Major Refurbishment works being carried out to an original building.

A typical refurbishment and completed building, combining small commercial premises, and modern living accommodation.

Me discussing site plans in the office with a Building Society Surveyor, the office staff thought that it was me arranging my pension.

Work in progress on a typical office and showroom project.

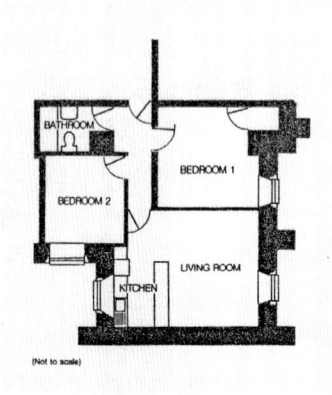

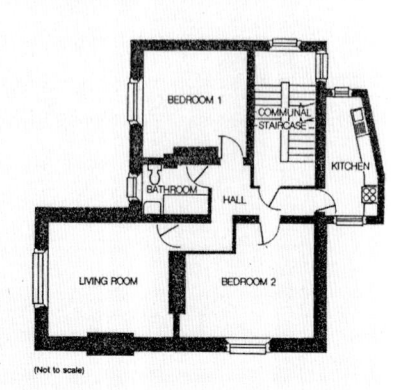

Front page of Brochure of Church Conversion.

Foundation works in progress within the Church Building.

Ground and First Floors, within the Church Building.

*Brickwork, and Blockwork progressing to form the
individual flats.*

Brickwork progressing upwards, ready for the next floor.

The buyers of these flats at Scawfell Terrace will have a special opportunity of appreciating the skill and thought embodied in the design and conversion These are unusually spacious and luxurious flats, and comprise of a large lounge/dining room generously sized bedrooms, ultra modern kitchens which are fitted with superb floor and wall units, built-in oven, hob and extractor hood. The bathroom suites are all in an Indian Ivory shade of colour and are of the very latest design, the wall to the bathrooms are attractively part tiled to harmonise with the sanitary ware.

There is full central heating, with the most popular system of all, hot water radiators with the modern small bore plumbing and an economical, trouble free, gas fired boiler. The whole flat is tastefully decorated all internal woodwork in white gloss, white ceilings and the walls decorated with Magnolia emulsion paint contrasting with the sober richness of the sapele Mahogany flushed doors. All living areas, halls, bedrooms and bathrooms are fully carpeted, kitchens with vinyl sheet. An entry phone is fitted for added security.

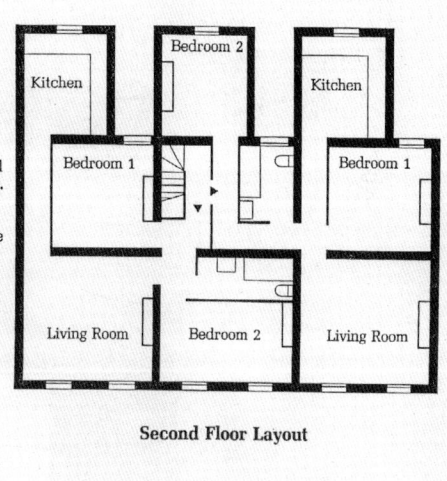

Second Floor Layout

Part brochure of three original Terrace Houses, Converted across the buildings so as to provide good spacious Two bedroom accommodation.

New 1 & 2 Bedroom Flats

Set amongst the trees and landscaped lawns, these elegant yet unobtrusive flats stand out as exceptional dwellings, and must surely be the ideal purchase for the first time buyer seeking a property at a modest price. As one and two bedroom units they offer superb well set out interiors with spacious living/dining areas.

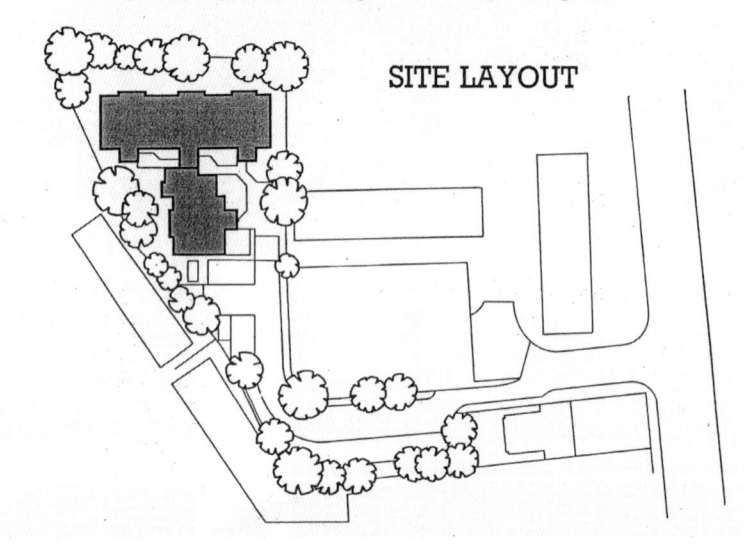

SITE LAYOUT

Front page of Brochure of One and Two Bedroom New Build Flats.

TYPICAL 1 BEDROOM FLAT

- Lounge/Diner
- Kitchen
- Bedroom

TYPICAL 2 BEDROOM FLAT

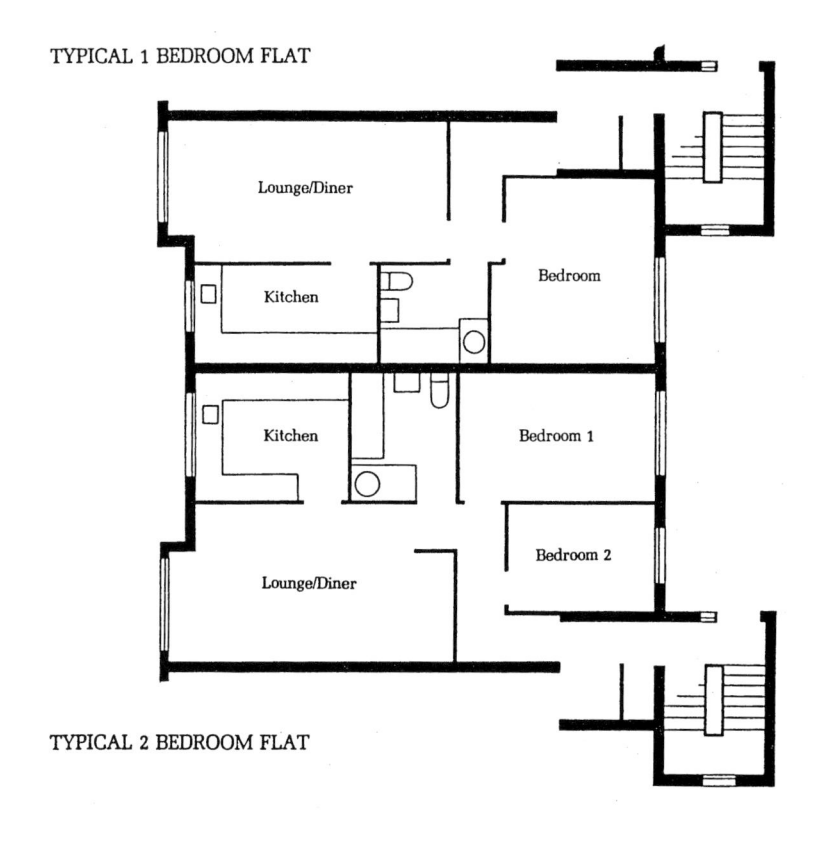

- Kitchen
- Bedroom 1
- Bedroom 2
- Lounge/Diner

Your 100% Mortgage is already arranged subject to status

Our Typical Layouts of New Build One, and Two Bedroom Flats, showing that 100% Mortgages already arranged, S.T.S, Through my newly formed Finance Company.

1988 / 89, the property market started to collapse, so I decided to shut down the major development side of the business, and hold on to the investment properties, this was carried out very successfully, and towards the end of 1988, after nearly six years of building up the Estates Agency business chain, which had grown to 10 offices throughout North and East London, the best way forward was to sell the offices one by one to maximise the best deals, I sold the last office to a National Company, just before the collapse, it was not because I knew what was about to come, but just good timing, and I was out, and in a good cash position.

In 1988, through to 1990, most of the property market had collapsed, Banks, and Building Societies, were placing properties in the auction rooms just to recoup some money back, any future deals had to be on a cash basis, as Banks were not in a lending mood.

I continued to build up the investment side of the business, and on one occasion I remember very well, I was in an auction room that I visited quite often, during the early afternoon, I had already purchased three properties, when an auction lot that I was interested in came up, it was a block containing 2 vacant lock up shops, and 2 occupied flats, the auctioneer read out the details, and started by saying "lets start at £15,000," not a sound from the room, he then said "lets start at £12, 000", still no response, next came £10,000, still nothing, he then said in his usual way "lets start at £8,000, I dont mind where we start, its where we finish", still nothing, no bids, at this time I raised my catalogue, the auctioneer quickly saw my bid, any advance on £8,000, nothing was heard, he then continued £8,000 for the first time, £8,000 for the second time, sold for £8,000, I was delighted – I still have that block of property, the flats are fully let, one of the vacant shops has since been converted into a two bedroom flat and has remained fully let, and the other lock up shop has been let on three yearly leases with upward only rent reviews ever since, when I look back, I think, what a good deal that was.

Even today, when I have completed a deal, I still look upwards, and say "good deal Grandad", in some way, I feel that he still hears me.

During the early part of the 1990's, I was approached by a Director of the Merchant Bank that had been so supportive to me over the previous years, he wanted me to work for the Bank on a consultancy basis one or two days per week, and to work along side my own activities, the work consisted of attending various department meeting, and advising the recovery department of the best way forward to maximise a return on the monies lent by the bank.

I would carefully analyse all the documents, visit the properties, and prepare a report, which would say, either build out the project, or sell, and recoup as much as possible., if the decision was to build out the property, or development, it would be my job to deal with the schedule of works, obtain contractors tenders, supervising all the works, and finally, advising on the sale of the properties, which included liaising with selling agents, if it was decided to foreclose on the deal, I would make a visit, prepare a full report and close down the site or property, with all the required notices. I believe that I was chosen for this task, because of my long previous experience, of which the bank were only to well aware of, my consultancy lasted about two years, after which most of the banks property deals that were in trouble, and had been allocated to me, had been cleared from the banks loan book.

In October 1993 I was admitted into the Middlesex Hospital in the West End of London, to have a triple heart by-pass, together with a L.I.M.A. I was told that this was a further by-pass placed directly into the heart, which is some times carried out whilst the by-pass operations are being carried out, the operation was carried out successfully, I remained in hospital for about 10 days, each day Pearl would come and visit me, and as she did not drive, she made the journey by bus, not a very pleasant journey, and seemed to take ages, but firstly, Pearl had to collect all the post from the office, and bring it to me at the hospital to go through, this of course did not please the doctors or nurses at the time, but business had to go on.

I did suffer a set back within a few weeks after the operation, this was caused by fluid in the heart and lungs, but the doctors were able to prescribe medication, which I have to take for the rest of my life.

When I returned to the hospital for a check up, I asked the Consultant if my heart was now softer in any way, he quickly told me that my heart was still as hard as before any operation, such re-assurance.

FREEMASONRY

When I was about 13 years old my Grandad Robinson took my Mum and myself to a Freemasons Ladies night, - the President of the Festival, was another Great Uncle, he was aunt Violet's husband, Mum looked beautiful in her evening gown, I wore a dinner suit for the first time complete with black tie (dicky bow) this was my first insight into Freemasonry, which I was very impressed.

The Robinson side of the family had always been very involved in Freemasonry going back to before the end of the 19th Century, my Grandfather, his father, and his brothers were founder members of quite a few Lodges many years ago, in fact my Great Uncle Sidney was initiated into the Warner Lodge on the 9th December 1902, being the 78th member to join the Warner Lodge, – Warner Lodge was founded by the Warner family who were very large property developers in the Walthamstow and surrounding areas at the turn of the 19th - 20th Century, and their Company 'Warner Estates' is still a very large property company today, in fact Courteney Warner was a well known figure and was knighted a few years later, he was Senior Warden of the Lodge when Great Uncle Sidney joined, perhaps, this is why Great Uncle Sidney joined that particular lodge with a common property interest and connection, Great Uncle Sidney became master of Warner Lodge in October 1909, and was appointed Prov JGD in 1911, at a later date Great Uncle Sidney became a founder member of the Forum Lodge, which was Consecrated on the 20th July 1911, and he became Master of the Forum Lodge in October 1912, and Treasurer for a number of years before retiring to become Honorary Member in 1921, he had

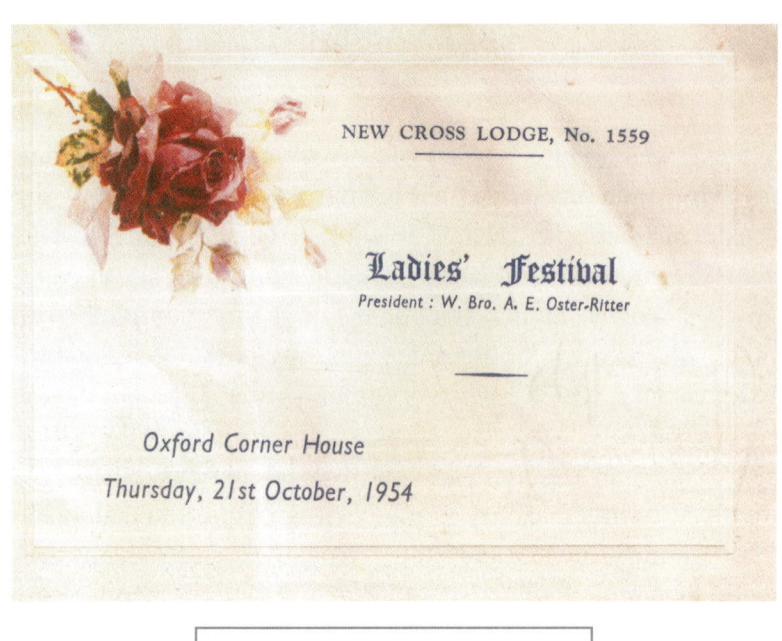

Copy of the Freemason's Ladies Festival invitation, that I attended in 1954. The President was my Great Aunt Violet's Husband.

138

My Mum, and Grandad, with me in my dinner suit, going to my first Masonic Ladies Night.

obtained the rank of LGR., PPGD, Prin G.Soj, at a meeting in February 1934, congratulations were sent to Great Uncle Sidney from the Lodge on hearing that the King had conferred Great Uncle Sidney with the honour of Knighthood.

On the 14th December 1912, my Grandad was Initiated into the Forum Lodge, by the Master who was – Great Uncle Sidney, and over the next few years they became founders members of quite a few lodges, one particular Lodge was the Rectitude Lodge in 1925, and the first master was Great Uncle George who had obtained the rank of PGD, he was also one of Grandad's brothers, in addition to being Lodge members they were all members of Royal Arch Chapters.

My Grandad said when I was young that he would arrange for me to become a Freemason, but I would have to wait until I became 21 years old, unfortunately my Grandad died before I reached 21 years, but after many years I eventually became a Freemason, and on the evening of my Initiation into a Lodge, and after all those years I felt my Grandad's hand holding mine as he had done all those years ago when I was a child, I felt him standing there beside me, a very strange, but good feeling, perhaps he really was there fulfilling a promise that he had made to a small boy all those years before, I like to think so.

After a few years 7 in all, and after serving in the various offices of the Lodge, I finally became Master of the Lodge the year was 2000, a new millennium, and another ambition achieved.

Myself in Freemason's Craft Regalia.

My Grandad Robinson, in his Freemason's Craft Regalia.

Myself in Chapter Regalia.

My Grandad Robinson in his Chapter Regalia.

MARK (My Nephew)

Quite recently Pearl and myself were invited to Mark's birthday party, during the evening there were speeches, when it came to Marks turn he started and thanked his wife, and his two girls, and then his Mum and Dad, then came a thank you to his Uncle Eric (me), he thanked me for helping him and training him over the years, I replied that I did not want thanking, the thanks was clearly shown by his achievements.

When Mark was about 14 years old and during his school holidays, he asked if he could come and work with me, of which he did, when he left school he worked for me full time, I started to teach him as I was taught, on one occasion I took him to a house that I had purchased in Tottenham, I told him to strip out the house ready for a conversion, he knew what to do as he had done it many times before, which included taking out all the fire places, built in cupboards, staircase balastrades, doors etc, I left him to it, as I could trust Mark to work without any supervision, he was, and still is, a very good and enthusiastic worker, when I returned the next day, I went into the property, which by then had been completely stripped with rubble, and debris all over the place, Mark was beginning to clear up, I said to Mark, go down stairs and check the number on the front door of the house, this he did, and shouted back to me that it was number 5, – Number 5, I said, it should be number 15, – well Mark looked at the mess throughout the house and I am sure he went very white, I smiled, and said, NO it should be number 5, but as a lesson Mark, always check at least twice, to make sure, – a lesson that I was taught, and Mark has never forgotten, and still talks about it, I wonder how many times he has used the lesson on his own workmen.

After a while, Mark continuing to work on my own development sites, and I put him to work with my best Site Agent, Mark was not very pleased at the time, as this was hard training, but says now that he learnt such a lot from that Site Agent.

Towards the end of the 1980's, I sold Mark a flat in Tottenham, Mark worked on the flat, and eventually let the flat and had his own first tenant, after a short time, Mark purchased another flat in the area, but this time, he completely refurbished the flat, he worked very hard on the project, not an easy task for a young man, who worked long hours, instead of going out with his mates etc, but it paid off, he sold the flat, and he was now on his way.

Over the years, Mark has always been very close to me, and now has his own Building Company, he has carried out refurbishment works for one of my Companies, over the years, and has since gone on to refurbishment works in the West End of London, and has made a great success, and he now has a substantial Building Company, including a few properties in his own portfolio.

Mark is very special to me, almost a Son, and I am so very proud of him and his achievements, he says that I taught him well, how to survive, and juggle finances, and how to succeed, I, of course, take that as a great compliment, but Mark has worked so very hard to achieve his goal, and what he now has, – it does seem strange, that Mark being my nephew (Mark is Pearl's Sister Eileen's son), no gene connection, but this has continued with an uncle and nephew relationship, that started in my family over 100 years before. In fact, my Grandad employed his nephew Sonny, my uncle

Alfred worked for his uncle Sidney, I worked with my Uncle's Alfred, and Lewis, and then Mark worked for me.

Having just written the above paragraph, regarding uncles, when I was young, and working for uncle Alfred, I asked him for some wages, he said "what do you want money for", I said because I dont have any, he replied, "no never will have", I told him many years later, that his remark all those years ago, made me think to prove him wrong, he laughed, and said that he was pleased that I had listened.

Another occasion with uncle Alfred was when I was about 15 years old, uncle Alfred gave me a black eye for being cheeky to aunt Rose, and himself, but after many years I told him that I deserved it, and that was all part of growing up.

All of Pearl's brothers worked for me over a period of time, and most of my nephews on Pearl's side of the family, but Mark was the only one to stay the test of time.

Pearl's Dad also worked for me over a long period, we got on very well he was the first person that I ever called dad, and we would have long conversations together at lunch times and when Pearl and myself would visit, he was quite a learned person, and we would discuss history etc, he was for some unknown reason very knowledgeable about the boxer uprisings in China, – on some occassions I would take him to 'Cookes' eel shop in Dalston, East London, he really loved stewed eels, like myself, his own sons did not like eels, and would never take him. I wonder now why I got on so well with him, he was quite a comical person, on one occassion we had to take a piano to Wood Green in the back of my van, when we stopped at traffic lights in Tottenham, Dad would start playing the piano in the back of the van completely invisible from the outside, (Dad was quite good at playing the piano) people passing would start to look around where was this music coming from, when the lights changed, we would drive away, and the music stopped, next set of lights, and again the music would start, same thing where was this music coming from.

Pearl's Mum was a truly loveable lady, who had a very hard life bringing up a large family on a small income, but she managed very well in her way, the only problem I had with Pearl's mum was that I was deprived of the usual mother-in-law jokes, as none of them seemed appropriate, I got on so very well with Pearl's mum, and loved her dearly, – again, what a lucky person I was to have such loving in laws.

RETURN TO SCHOOL

In 2004, I decided to pay a visit to my old school, after all it was 50 years since I had left, I made the necessary arrangements with what is now called the headteacher, in my days that would have been the headmaster, however, the arrangements were made, so I set off with Pearl as usual by my side, we were both very well greeted by the headteacher, and two of the older children, who I understand had various duties within the school, like for example, one was the editor of the school magazine, we were shown over the school, much had changed since I was last there, quite a few new extensions to the building, but of course the timber huts that we used as classrooms had disappeared, and replaced by permanent brick buildings, most of the corridors were still there, including the headmasters office.

The class rooms were now very different, gone was the blackboards, chalk, and the board rubber, that I of course remember so well, we had to duck, or move very quickly out of the way, if chalk, or the board rubber was thrown at us by the teacher, if we were not paying attention, I must say that our teachers were very good shots, the class rooms now had up to date computer screens on the walls, which had replaced the blackboards, I was shown how these computer screens worked, such a great improvement from my day.

Some of the rooms were still familiar, I was shown into the gymnasium, this was the same gym as I remembered, the walls still had the original wall bars, that I had used, the ropes were still hanging from the ceiling, I would assume that these had been replaced, various vaulting horses were around the room, – but what was missing? of course the boxing ring, which had been so prominent in my days,

I enquired, and was told told that boxing was now not allowed in the school, I do believe that this must be a mistake, perhaps if the boxing ring was returned to schools, perhaps, it would help in reducing the amount of bullying, as it did in our days.

I feel that the teachers work very hard at their jobs, but appear to be held back, firstly, it appears that discipline has gone, the type of lessons are all so different, very little time spent on such lessons as history, and general mathematics, like simple adding and subtracting, but of course this is only my opinion, and, as they say, I am now one of the grumpy old men.

What I did particularly notice is that the various house names from the classes had disappeared, this was very important to us in our days, it provided us with competition, competition between the various houses, in any subjects, competition was a great provider in building character of the children, sadly, this does not appear to be there any more.

Towards the end of the visit we had a question and answer time, with the children, this was very interesting, but so different from 50 years ago, – after thanking all the staff and children that we had met, we had our photos taken for the school magazine, Pearl and I left, I was so pleased to have visited my old school, the school, I, for one, will always be grateful for the basic education that school had provided to me.

VISIT TO LOCAL SCHOOL

In 2005 – being 60 years after the end of the second world war I was asked by a local school in Cambridgeshire, to visit and talk to the children about life for children growing up during the war in London, I was very pleased to accept, I was also very impressed by the way the children had made various models of war time things such as Anderson Shelters, and Public Shelters etc, they had collected a large number of old photos, and had made a good exhibition.

When I met with the children, I was very surprised to note that the ages were from 6 to 11 years, I could not believe that some of the poems that the children had written were produced by such young children. I started my talk about life in wartime in the East End of London, the children were so interested, and may I say so were the teachers, at the end of the talk, I asked if they had any questions, – one small boy asked did I ever go scrumping, where had he heard such a phrase, I replied, sometimes, if we could find any fruit left on so few trees, of course this was quite new to children living in a country area, full of fruit trees, but then had to come a fuller explanation of why so few fruit trees in London's East End, another question, and quite hard to answer, "Why did the German's bomb us", I replied as best as I was able, which was greeted by the class with a big "But We Won".

What seemed strange to me was that the teachers were also asking questions, and saying that their Grandfathers had told them about their time in the war, this made me stop and think, but of course, these teachers are the grandchildren of the chaps that fought in that war, I was so pleased to have been given the opportunity, and to experience, that this school was in fact teaching part of our history.

Pearl and myself cutting our cake at our 25th wedding Anniversary in 1985.

ANNIVERSARIES

Pearl and me held our 25th wedding anniversary party at the Royal Chase Hotel in Enfield, in 1985, which was well attended, and with the arrival of Pearl's aunt Connie, and Pearl's Cousins who had travelled all the way from Australia, our 40th wedding anniversary was held in Bournemouth over a whole week end, with family and friends, and in 2006, I arranged a 70th birthday party for Pearl, it was held in the Prince Regent Hotel in Chigwell Essex, in February, although Pearl's birthday was in fact on the 21st December 2005, but with the holiday period at that time of the year, it may have been difficult for some members of the family to attend.

The party was very well attended by most of our joint families, what a great pleasure for us all to get together, – and with our close friends, some of our families and friends stayed, and made a complete week end of it, we all enjoyed a great meal, which was followed by speeches, to Pearl, which were quite moving, the entertainment for the first part of the evening was by an exceptionally good Elvis impersonator, great fun, of course, Rock-n-Roll was in fact the type of music that we had enjoyed in our earlier years, especially Pearl, who even now is still a very good dancer, later in the evening there was dancing which went on until the early hours.

We do expect to hold our 50th wedding anniversary in 2010, God willing, ... the venue at the moment is still unknown.

Pearl and myself at our 25th wedding anniversary, taken with Pearl's youngest brother.

Pearl and myself at our 40th wedding anniversary.

Pearl and myself at Pearl's 70th Birthday Party.

My first intentions when I decided to write this book, was to write a complete chapter about my Mum, but this did not work out, as clearly my mum features throughout the book.

Mum towards the end of her life was in a nursing home for 4 years suffering from Alzheimers, and over what appeared to be a short time she deteriorated over the months, and was admitted into Whipps Cross hospital in East London, and on the night of the 12th January 2005, she died peacefully in her sleep, with Pearl and myself by her side, she had now joined my Dad , and her family that had all gone before her.

Mum had just passed her 89th birthday, what a sad end to a lady that had been so strong and determined all of her life to gradually go back to childhood ways, but of course that was Alzheimers.

Within a three year period I had lost my two uncles (Lewis and Alfred), who were like brothers to me, and my Mum, it appeared at the time that my immediate family had been wiped out, – but of course there were still other member of our close family, my cousin Gillian, said to me "we are all part of an extended family", a true blessing that I have had all of my life.

Words seem to be such an inadequate way to express one's emotions, and true feelings, – but what else is there ?

The deeper I became mentality and even emotionally involved in the progress of writing my own family history, the stronger grew, and not an unpleasant feeling, that my ancestors seemed to be at my side as I wrote about them.

The last photograph of myself with my uncles – Alfred left hand side, – me in the middle – Lewis right hand side, of course a very treasured photograph.

Quite recently, I suffered from a very painful episode with pain in my mouth, this was so bad, that I had to visit the local hospital, Pearl and I sat in the waiting room, after a very short while, a doctor called out **Mr YARKOB**, I rose and went into see him, – he said "did I pronounce your name correctly" I said yes, if you were in Germany, he replied by saying that he had trained with the British Army in Germany as a Doctor, and said that this was the way he pronounced the name in Germany, he asked me if I was Jewish, I said that I was not going to tell him, – he continued to treat me, gave me a prescription for some pills, and said see my G.P. the next day, as I was leaving, he said "Happy Hanukkah" I just turned and smiled.

Oh, and another thing whilst I remember;

I was told that most good books, films, play's etc, must have some of the following: – Poverty – Hardship – Sex – Success – most of the above are included within the book, except the sex, unfortunately, for the reader, the sex life of Eric, is a very private matter.

During my life I was to suffer a further two financial disasters, probably because I had taken my eye of the ball, but again, my mind was engaged into action, and I overcame the difficulties, nothing better than a sudden turn in the market place, or general conditions, to make you stop, and think, when you are down, the only way is up, so when the property crash came in the early 1990's, I was well prepared, I would emphasise that any success does not all ways come easy ...

I believe that because of my very early training all those years ago, I have been able to have the staying power, and can cope in any crises, I am a self confessed workaholic, very rarely go on holiday, could work happily seven days a week, up to 16 hours a day, if a deal needs doing, I still find it extremely hard to relax, but I now finish in my office most days by 6.30 pm, those who know me understand me for what I am capable of, – and not for any vanity.

I still believe that there are some really good deals to be had, and money to be made, the opportunities are enormous today, but it requires a certain type of person to make it.

In 1997, I purchased a large detached house in a very pretty part of Cambridgeshire, Mark carried out a complete refurbishment of the house, and Pearl and me moved into the house in February 1998, the house is set behind its own electronic gates, within an acre of grounds, with its own tennis court, quite a different place from our first two rented rooms in Stamford Hill, I suppose, when I look back, and think to where Pearl and myself are now, I am sure that my Grandad, and my Dad would be proud of our achievements.

I am now 68 years old, I still work, and run a successful property investment company, I wont say what my personal worth is, but one of my companies properties are valued in excess of £30 million pounds, I still run my finance company, not so busy now, but still lending on a smaller scale than years ago.

My Residential Property Portfolio now spreads from Southsea on the South Coast, through Kent – Berkshire – Middlesex – London both North, and of course, East London, – Essex – Suffolk – Hertfordshire – Cambridgeshire – Nottinghamshire – and Lincolnshire.

Not bad, for Just A Boy From London's East End, raised by a single parent, and second generation immigrant on my fathers side.

What of my future: ...   Who Knows: ...

Retirement, I dont think so, after all my Great uncle Sidney, was still controlling his many interest in his office up to the day before his death, ... my Grandad, was still involved in deals just before he died, ... Sir Charles Clore, was still dealing up to the time he died, ... my friends, and colleagues are still working long after retirement age,

Retirement is a time for enjoyment, working is my enjoyment, as far as I am concerned: ...

ALL WORK AND NO PLAY MAKES MONEY

Strange when I look back on my life, at the different roads that I may have taken and I now say: ...

What If: ...   My Grandad had not intervened at a early part of my life?

What If: ...   My Dad had not been killed in the war?

What If: ...   My Mum had not been the type of person that she was?

What If: ...   I had chosen the criminal way of life?

What If: ...   I had chosen an Army Career?

What If: ...   I had a different uncaring family?

What If: ...   I had stayed in the night I met Pearl?

I dont really want to think about any of these alternatives, and I thank God, for what I did, and do have, I dread to think of my life without Pearl by my side.

Room for thought,--- I would emphasis that this is only my opinion, as I have already said, I am now one of the grumpy old men, but as a general remark on today's education, I would comment on four items set out below;

(a) Common Sense. Seems to have completely disappeared.

(b) Disciple Now appears to be non- existent.

(c) Respect. Appears to have gone forever.

(d) Morals. Just look at the teenage pregnancies today, I am told that this Country has the highest in Europe.

Education, I hear from time to time from employers, that the majority of school leavers who apply for jobs, cannot even do the simplest of adding and subtracting numbers, struggle with English, such as completing an application form for a job, letter writing etc, – what a difference from our schooling, – I wonder what children will write in 50 or so years time about their schooling, if of course they can write.

ACKNOWLEDGEMENTS

I am extremely grateful to the Royal Green Jackets Museum for their very kind permission to quote from their own book,

"The King's Royal Rifle Corps ... The 60th Rifles
A Brief History: 1755 to 1965"

Which is reproduced on pages 100–101

Also Lieutenant General Sir Christopher Wallace KBE DL for his kind words wishing me every success in completing this book.

****

I am also very grateful for permission to reproduce illustrations provided by Walthamstow Historical Society on pages 18, 21, 22, 23, 24, 25

All other illustrations are from originals held by the Author.

****

NOTES

NOTES

NOTES

NOTES